STRATEGIES
FOR SURVIVING
BULLYING AT WORK

Evelyn M. Field

www.
AUSTRALIANACADEMIC**PRESS**
.com.au

First published in 2011
Australian Academic Press
32 Jeays Street
Bowen Hills Qld 4006
Australia
www.australianacademicpress.com.au

National Library of Australia Cataloguing-in-Publication entry

Author:	Field, Evelyn.
Title:	Strategies for surviving bullying at work / Evelyn Field.
ISBN:	9781921513817 (pbk.)
	9781921513824 (ebook)
Subjects:	Bullying in the workplace.
	Bullying in the workplace--Prevention.
	Harassment.
	Discrimination in employment.
	Discrimination in employment--Prevention.
Dewey Number:	331.133

Disclaimer
While every effort has been taken in the preparation of the material in this book, the author and publisher shall have neither liability nor responsibility to any person or entity with respect to any loss or damage caused or alleged to be caused directly by the information contained herein. The purpose of this book is to inform, educate, assist and provide some ways of coping.

It does not seek to recommend any particular course of action, rather to outline options and likely outcomes. The ideas, procedures and suggestions contained in this book are not intended as a substitute for consulting a psychologist, doctor or lawyer. All matters regarding your health require proper medical supervision and all matters concerning your legal rights require proper legal assistance.

Cartoons by Matt Mawson. Cover designed by Maria Biaggini.
Typeset in Adobe Garamond 12pt by Australian Academic Press.

This book makes for invaluable reading as it helps to build the necessary self-help strategies and resilience to effectively tackle the different stages of workplace bullying.

Professor Mona O'Moore, Associate Professor in the School of Education
Founder and Director of the Anti-Bullying Research and Resource Centre
Trinity College, Dublin

Evelyn Field's stellar contribution to the field of workplace bullying is to pull from the research literature, from her practice as counsellor and therapist, and from her own hard experience, eminently practical lessons for how to respond to the problem in ways that actually make things better. She is too wise a lady to fall for panaceas or to pander to pipe dreams. She is attentive to evidence, sober and methodical. What is more, her prose sparkles with clarity and punch — and for that reason, is genuinely helpful to people brutalised at work.

Kenneth Westhues, PhD
Professor Emeritus of Sociology & Legal Studies
University of Waterloo, Canada

This is an important book, a sophisticated and comprehensive primer on managing workplace bullying, the next generation of books on this topic. This book moves beyond the victim perspective for those who have experienced bullying and provides sound advice for healing and rebuilding after bullying. If you have experienced work-place bullying and are struggling to recover, you must read this book. If you are an HR professional, you must consider this book your textbook. Even psychologists and other counselling professionals often fail to grasp the enormous impact of bullying behaviours or the skills required to defuse or reduce bullying behaviours.

Pat Ferris, MSW, RSW, MSc, PhD
Partner, Calgary Psychology Group

There are so many difficulties of living in our modern era due to terrorism, economic and natural disasters. At least we have a solution for making the quality of our life at the workplace better. This new book from Evelyn Field can really help us in coping with bullying at work. This is the first book I know which really teaches us and provides simple, useful strategies to help anyone block or cope with bullying behav-iours. As in many areas of life, the essence of resilience at work is emotional wellbeing, effective communication skills and social support.

Dan Zakay, Professor of Cognitive Psychology
Head, Graduate Program in Organizational Development and Consulting
The Inter-Disciplinary Center, Herzeliya, Israel

Evelyn Field writes with the clarity and knowledge of the truly experienced clinician. She goes straight to the facts in a no-nonsense style, making her message clear to everyone. Workplace bullying is all too common, and the effect is potentially devastating for the victim. Evelyn provides you with the tools to empower yourself, reflect on your situa-tion, understand what is happening to you and how to counter the adverse effects to your health and wellbeing. *Strategies for Surviving Bullying at Work* is a great example of that noble tradition of helping people help themselves. We highly recommend it.

Rune Raudeberg, psychologist and Nils Mageroy, MD/PhD
Jobbfast — Research Clinic on Trauma and Psychosocial Stressors at Work
Haukeland University Hospital, Bergen, Norway

Bullying in the workplace is a game to a few and a health hazard to many. For me, the keywords in this book are 'respect' and 'responsibility'. This second half will help all parties involved in a bullying episode to deal with the situation effectively and appropriately.

Professor Michael Sheehan
Head, Department of Management, Business School
University of Glamorgan, Wales

In her new book, Evelyn Field provides a survival guide for those who have been bullied, for those who are being bullied and those who may be bullied in the future. The survival strategy espoused by Evelyn Field is the process I have used. First, the strategy involves detachment where the target becomes an observer of their own problem. They observe their problem through the eyes of others, including bystanders, management, and even the bully. Detachment is important because it permits analytical thought and not emotional thought. No bully is blocked through emotion. Second, the strategy of survival is based on the principle that your problem is not unique. One in six employees is bullied, and each target can learn from every other target. Bullies use a template, and every template can be inverted. Third, successful survival depends on rebuilding relations, with others and with yourself. To know and support yourself has no greater imperative than for those who have been bullied. Evelyn Field provides the evidence and the analysis needed to block bullies, to invert their bullying, and to survive. Evelyn has blown the whistle on bullying.

Dr Kim Sawyer, Associate Professor,
University of Melbourne

Your book is like a lifeline. It has identified all the mechanisms of both bullying and being bullied. Although at times some things pertinent to my own case were confronting, hitting many a nerve, it was comforting to have had my experiences validated. I'm not crazy, or paranoid, or incompetent, or overly sensitive ... I was a healthy, normal, strong person who got ground into the dirt where I now exist as a lumpy, greasy residue. I'm trying so hard to pick up the pieces and put myself back together again, but some of the bits are missing, never to be replaced.

Linda
Workplace bully survivor

I found your book so accurate that it's difficult to read without taking time to digest and reflect ... So many patient accounts in your book relate to my experience and the devastating implications for my career and life since leaving. Thank you for your professional contribution to this area. The first eight months after leaving I lived at my local library and read everything available that relates to this experience. I believe your book to be the first truly authentic understanding of this issue and its implications.

Brad
Workplace bully survivor

To Mia, my first grandchild,
who by filling a void from the past,
is helping me build a new life.

'If I am not for myself, who will be for me?
But if I am only for myself, who am I?
If not now, when?'

Rabbi Hillel
Jewish scholar & theologian (30 BC–9 AD)

Contents

Preface...ix

INTRODUCTION
The secrets of relating 1

CHAPTER 1
Building your social and emotional resilience at work 3

CHAPTER 2
Strategy 1: Regulate your feelings 27

CHAPTER 3
Strategy 2: Understand the reasons 51

CHAPTER 4
Strategy 3: Revalue and restore your identity....................................69

CHAPTER 5
Strategy 4: Use effective communication skills 85

CHAPTER 6
Strategy 5: Protect and empower yourself 107

CHAPTER 7
Strategy 6: Use your support network 131

Conclusion 145

References 147

Bibliography...150

About the author 152

Acknowledgments 154

Preface

This book is an essential follow-up to my earlier volume, *Bully Blocking at Work*, although it can be read independently. Both books deal with the devastating effects on individuals of workplace bullying but, while Volume 1 focused on understanding the issue of workplace bullying, this book will empower individuals to care for themselves and others in bullying situations.

I have worked as a psychologist for over 30 years and helped many different types of clients, including targets of schoolyard bullying and victims of criminal trauma. Still to this day, every time I hear a workplace bullying story in my practice I am hit with a horrible feeling in the pit of my stomach. Most people are aware of the problems of bullying at school, but very few realise the extent or the impact of bullying on adults at work.

Workplace bullying is a serious psychological issue that deserves the utmost attention by the health management and human resources sectors. Many mental health professionals fail to assess symptoms accurately. It is no wonder. There is little education for those treating the problem, or for those in a position to prevent it. When workplace bullying is ignored, or dealt with in ignorance, it can spiral out of control, harming both the individuals involved and the productivity and reputation of the organisation in which it occurs.

Bullying involves the regular abuse of power. It cannot occur where both people feel equally powerful — that is called a conflict. It can include a wide number of behaviours, ranging from banter through denial of professional opportunities to physical violence. Sometimes it appears innocuous or petty, and the targets of bullying might feel uncertain about whether they are being bullied. You can be bullied from all directions — by managers, clients, customers, peers, or even subordinates. Both men and women can be bullies and targets of bullying. If you feel confused, humiliated, powerless and threatened at work, it is likely you are being bullied.

My desire to teach survival and resilience when dealing with difficult, mean or cruel people was influenced by my family history: many of my family were killed at the hands of the Nazis during World War ll. Much later, my daughter Miriam died in tragic circumstances. These compelling circumstances, plus my own shyness, led me to think deeply about the ways people relate and connect. As a result, I developed a social skills model that helps people care for themselves and others. I have used this model for many years to help children who have been bullied at school. Now in this book I have adapted it to assist targets of workplace bullying.

In *Bully Blocking at Work*, I considered strategies for workplaces to effectively manage bullying. It is up to employers to provide a safe workplace and there are clear actions they can take. However, after many years of research, education and intervention into schoolyard bullying, I realise we have yet to significantly reduce that behaviour. We will be equally ineffective in reducing workplace bullying if we leave it to others to act. If you are a target of bullying, you can help yourself, with support from this book and also from medical, legal and psychology specialists where needed. My focus is on teaching social and emotional resilience to empower people — helping you to develop skills to deal with the ups and downs of life. In this book, I provide the six secrets of relating that will give you that power.

The secrets of relating

Our ancestors lived in tribes; when they faced pain, distress or hardship, they were supported and cared for by others. Today we have the same need for strong networks to survive and yet many people are socially isolated. How do we relate, connect and create networks in this world, where the tribe is not a given? This question has become the core my work and my model — helping human beings to become social beings again.

My model of social relating is based upon my personal and professional experience. It helps you relate to and care for yourself more effectively and to learn the skills of relating to and caring for others. It helps you deal with difficult people. This model has been used successfully to help victims of trauma and people with relationship difficulties of all kinds, including the particular difficulty of protecting yourself from bullies. This model was originally published in *There's More to Life Than Sex and Money* (Johnston & Calwell, 1998). It is the core of *Bully Busting* (Field, 1999) and *Bully Blocking* (Field, 2007).

I have used a butterfly as the image for this model of relating. It has special meaning for me because the group Compassionate Friends, which supports parents who have lost a child, uses it as their symbol. My daughter Miriam, who died tragically young, also loved these colourful insects. Butterflies are often used as a symbol of metamorphosis or change, a concept which offers possibility to many people suffering in toxic relationships or enduring trauma.

The model is in two parts. The left wing of the butterfly deals with the way you relate to your inner core, your feelings. It helps you to understand why things happen to you and also to rebuild

your self-esteem and learn to value yourself again. The right wing of the butterfly shows you how to relate to others, using basic verbal and non-verbal communication skills, empowering you to confront or block difficult people and to use your support networks. The six labels on the butterfly refer to the six secrets for surviving bullying at work. The butterfly model is based on the concept of taking action. Regardless of who did what to whom, where and when, you must accept responsibility for caring for yourself because this is your life.

In the pages that follow, you will find quotes from many people I have worked with over the years. These are the genuine voices of bullies and their targets, managers, relatives, bystanders and friends. Sometimes it is the simple act of hearing another's pain and struggle that helps us take those important steps forward for our own survival. Remember though, if you feel too many traumatic memories or emotional stress are surfacing, you can always return to it later. This book is designed to give you long-term support, so read the parts that seem relevant now and return later to other parts.

CHAPTER ONE

Building your social and emotional resilience at work

❝*Although I was bullied by a psychopath, I hoped for years that I could return to work. Sometimes I still talk about what 'we do' there. Soon after I was forced out of work by a breakdown, the main bully was pushed out, another one moved out later, while a third one came and went, via the nepotism network. The lawyer promised justice through a common law claim, which was planned to take three years. Eight years after the bullying ended I went to court for a nightmarish three weeks. My employer was exonerated! My lawyer appealed. A year later, no evidence could place responsibility for bullying onto my employer! Ten years later I am still out of work, totally unemployable. I am forced to pick up the pieces of my life, too old to work, numerous health difficulties and no justice. My employer got rid of more bullies, they are doing more staff training and are more aware of the evils of bullying. I never received an apology, validation or justice.* ❞

Workplaces can be dirty, difficult, disgusting and sometimes dangerous. Ethics, etiquette and equality may be ignored and employees can be undervalued. Despite the need for specialised training and experience, cost of hiring and firing, or job shortages in some industries, employees are often treated no better than an empty carton — easy to bully out and replace. Those who are required and respected are lucky; however, in most workplaces bullying, like weeds or cobwebs, will be lurking around.

Bullying at work involves a variety of behaviours that involve the sustained abuse of power; it can come from any direction — a manager, colleague or someone below you. It affects more than half the work-place in some way and creates a toxic, unproductive working environment costing billions of dollars to employers and the general community with organisational and welfare costs. Although personality is often blamed despite there being no actual evidence, bullying is basically enabled and condoned by poor management practices (O'Moore & Crowley, 2011). It seems to be more common in some industries, such as health, welfare, education and hospitality.

Some people identify the bullying immediately and take effective action to report it and block the bully; or they may intuitively sense danger, and curl-up to protect themselves, like an echidna. Others realise that the bully is threatened, so they don't rock the boat and perhaps use flattery to undermine the bully's attacks, or they leave their workplace. Unfortunately, a few brave souls wait in hope for the bullying to stop, or for an apology, or a fair investigation process to materialise, leaving themselves open to continued attack. They appear 'vulnerable' if they react and retaliate, thereby inviting further abuse, while simultaneously risking further injury. Sadly, bystanders can also be physically and psychologically affected, and about one fifth will leave this job (Rayner, Howl, & Cooper, 2002).

Injury

Some people suffer a sudden injury such as a snapped tendon, others experience the slow pressure of muscle overuse and develop a repetitive strain injury, whereas most targets of bullying are appalled at how the slow build-up of subtle, toxic behaviours can injure them. Consequently, many can be physically, psychologically and socially injured for months or permanently.

When a person is diagnosed with a life-threatening illness like mesothelioma, most people are aware of the clinical evidence and accept that it was caused by long-term, repeated exposure to asbestos fibres — nothing else! However, despite recent evidence (Field, 2010b) that the constellation of symptoms diagnosed in victims of workplace bullying appear to be different to those in people suffering work-related stress, death of a parent or a redundancy, and could not be caused by anything apart from serious, traumatising workplace bullying, the victims are blamed and forced to provide legal proof of bullying, as if their symptoms would disappear when there is no legal evidence!

This lack of professional understanding means that victims are mistreated by their employer, the law and insurance companies; they are regarded as malingers or under-diagnosed and treated inappropriately, thereby delaying their recovery by many years and costing society millions of dollars.

Why does this happen?

Recent studies demonstrate that people who are seriously injured at work can experience anxiety, depression and, more significantly, posttraumatic stress disorder. This implies that the toxic consequences of going to a dysfunctional workplace has similar symptoms to being physically assaulted (Eisenberg, Lieberman, & Williams, 2003). However, most people realise that an assault is a criminal offence that will be treated seriously, yet the target of bullying may have little support except from a few friends, some of whom may abandon them when the going gets tough. Apart from states or countries where bullying is considered a crime, such as France or Victoria (Australia), the broken warriors of the workplace seldom receive validation or a sound, evidence-based, ethical diagnostic label! This has the unfortunate effect of injuring a victim even further.

What happens to a target's identity and relationships?

I have spent many years working with children as they encounter the ups and downs of adolescence — the whirlpool of changing emotions, slowly developing cognitive functions, sexual and social identity, body image and so on. While they journey through puberty to adolescence and early adulthood they encounter a metamorphosis based on challenges to their identity. Their key struggles are associated with 'Who am I?' and 'Where do I belong socially?'

The flip side is reflected in the challenges facing adults in the second half of their lives, such as menopause, reduced sexual and physical ability, ill-health, deteriorating cognitive functions. As the dreams of their youth disintegrate, they are forced to reinvent their identity to manage their aging body and mind.

Similarly, without realising it at the time, victims of bullying who are seriously injured, trying to exist without validation, and forced to undergo drawn-out medico–legal processes, will experience a critical, severe, sometimes crippling identity change. Thus workplace bullying impacts on victim's physical, emotional, social, sexual, and cognitive functions and most of all, their personality, or who they are and how they see themselves. In addition, bullying also injures the way others see targets, especially if they lose their career, social status and financial well-being. Therefore many targets feel social stigma, shame and humiliation upon losing their social position, and also lose their previous positive self-esteem.

Lutgen-Sandvik (2008, p. 116) stated that '… for persons who strongly identify with their jobs or professions, the experience can be devastating.' She believes that employees face intensive remedial identity work to manage these persistently stressful, traumatic and stigmatising organisa-tional experiences that can occur in at least three phases, including abuse onset, escalation and cessation. However, some will never recover to work again, thereby injuring their whole personality permanently.

Social connectedness

The stories victims relate show that most of them will reduce the number of people they can trust or socialise with at work and elsewhere. So at the next job they will be more cautious, less sociable and perhaps less avail-able to participate in teamwork. Those who are forced to leave work per-manently reduce their social relationships even more. Although they may maintain a few old friendships, they tend to interact less, and this can also apply to the extended family. In some cases, they make friends with those who are going through similar traumas — for example, via a support group — and then socialise where they feel very safe. However, some find that their ability to form relationships is so shattered that they can't chat and connect, participate socially, trust others and become intimate. Their lives become lonely and isolated. Many lose their sense of social belonging, which is necessary for survival.

Resilience

Resilience represents the skills and strategies required to deal with the 'ups and downs' of life. It is the ability to adjust to adversity in a positive or constructive manner, and consider all difficulties as a challenge. It involves a capacity to confront pain, suffering and trauma and know that it will eventually lessen. It is linked to the belief that it may take years to heal and that progress is based upon persistence, despite the setbacks. It is the skill of regarding the glass as half full, not half empty, and using one's perception to make the switch.

There is no value in spending the rest of your life bemoaning the lack of justice and opportunity. The sooner you take action to assist, protect and empower yourself to manage the bullying, whether or not you are successful, there will be less likelihood of symptoms developing now and a more serious injury later on. You can begin by being grateful for what you have; as Ferris (2010) says, develop an 'attitude of gratitude'.

How do you become resilient?

Michelle Slone (2010) from Tel Aviv University studied children who underwent daily rocket attacks and identified four of the most important factors for resilience. These include obtaining appropriate support, attributing meaning to the traumatic experience, developing self-efficacy and problem-solving skills, and improving self-esteem. These skills are also integrated within the treatment programs for victims of workplace bullying (Tehrani, 2001; AHG Klinik Berus (rehabilitation clinic], as cited in Einarson, Hoel, Zapf, & Cooper, 2011).

Thus it is vital that if you are being bullied, you protect yourself from any injury. You can build your personal strengths by developing strategies such as creating positive and nurturing professional relationships, maintaining positivity, developing emotional insight, achieving life balance, finding spirituality and becoming more reflective (Jackson, Firtko, & Edenborough, 2007).

This book is useful if you are at work and the bullying has just begun or is escalating, or when you have left work to find employment elsewhere; or if, unfortunately, you are too injured to work for a long period of time.

Turning points, and time to move on

When I have interviewed clients, many claim that they would have managed their bullying experiences and taken a different course of action had they realised how toxic and damaging the whole process can be. For example, they may have left, researched their legal rights, recorded all bullying incidents, not taken it personally, confronted the bully, obtained professional help, eliminated blind faith and trust from their managers, requested an independent witness to attend meetings, or gone as high as possible to the Board of Management. Many wished that they had known how difficult taking legal action, such as a common law claim, can be.

Thus, you need to find out your options the moment the bullying begins, and although you may not have access to a therapist who can ask the right question at the right time, you still need to ask yourself what you will need to experience in order to feel vindicated and decide if it is worth the fight. Then establish that moment in time when you will decide to end this arduous battle for justice. In other words, without cutting off a limb to escape, you need to decide when 'enough is enough', that you can't do any more and it is time to mourn and move on.

Challenge myths, get the facts

1. Bullies are bad

Most personalities are neither black or white, most are shades of grey. For example, some people can be bad in business, but give huge financial donations to charity. Many good people hurt others without realising it, such as the missionaries who brought disease to native populations, or senior executives who exclude women from equal jobs and salaries.

Similarly, most people don't intend to be annoying but may end up like the snorer in the next room, or the person who coughs loudly throughout a show.

Fact

Most managers and work colleagues do not realise that they are bullying you or others, and you may be able to use a variety of strategies to resolve this stressful relationship — for example, organise a time when you can chat about your feelings about their inappropriate behaviour, and collaborate to find a reasonable solution, or find out what you do to threaten or aggravate them; alternatively, reframe the problem as theirs and just do your job properly, while remaining neutral and detached.

2. Both genders are the same

Remember that men and women deal with bullying differently: boys support their boy's club, regardless of ethics and evidence, while women can be 'frenemies' who are 'nice' to your face, then bitch behind your back and betray your previous friendship.

Men often regard work as a hunting game and socialise in large packs. As their relationships are less intense, less intimate and more neutral, they have less information to misuse and less need for retaliation when sabotaged. They challenge you openly or explode privately and say 'That's business' and then press their reset button (see *Bully Blocking at Work*; Field, 2010).

Women are gatherers, accustomed to sharing and working together in small groups. They chat and gossip to build connections in an intense manner. They reveal more personal, private information but then turn upon one another when threatened, and can divulge toxic information. Women are more sensitive, thus they relive, review, recall and remember. They suffer for longer and are more traumatised when bullied.

Fact

Understand that your gender will affect how you manage the bullying and cope with your injuries.

3. Reality check

Generally, photographers tend to show the world as it is (although some photos are manipulated), whereas a painter shows the world according to his perceptions. Being bullied is a mind-blowing experience, catapulting you into foreign territory. Don't be clouded by your thoughts, beliefs and previous experiences, which can create a false picture. You need to prove your perceptions: Does the bully really want to hurt you or are they unaware of your distress? Are you exacerbating the bullying in some way, such as remaining in hostile territory, over-reacting, paralysed or threatening them in some manner?

Fact

Most bullies are insecure, many are incompetent, all have limited people skills and all are badly managed, but they can improve their relationships with mentoring. You need to investigate all available options and find more appropriate relating skills and strategies to manage the bullying (Crawshaw, 2000).

4. I'm not responsible

Many targets believe that as they did nothing to cause the bullying, it is *not* their responsibility to take any action. This is like saying, 'Although I broke my hip when I slipped on the banana peel in the corridor at work, the person who dropped it needs treatment!'

Fact

Although you may not be responsible for the bullying, you are responsible for your health and wellbeing. Regardless of whether you were involved directly or indirectly with bullying, you may have been injured and could need to take assertive action to protect and heal yourself, as others can't always help you. After all, your health and wellbeing is at risk of serious injury and you need to reduce any toxic impact where possible.

5. I don't need to take action

Sometimes disaster strikes without warning and there is nothing you can do to prevent it. At other times, although there are immediate, recognisable signs of doubt, disbelief or danger, it builds up slowly over a long period of time. Those employees who identify the bullying and take the best action at the time tend to be less affected.

Fact

Regardless of whether or not you followed your gut instinct and taken action is history. Now you need to activate your survival instinct and employ every means at your disposal to protect yourself from future harm. This 'attitude switch-shift' can save you from further injury. Remaining in a bullying workplace is like swimming in shark-infested waters. Taking action is recognition that your wellbeing, family and friends are more important than this job; not an admission of defeat or a sign of failure. Regard your future exit as a carefully planned military withdrawal, whenever it may occur. Then, although you may be phys-ically and intellectually employed, you can switch off emotionally. Your commitment and attachments will change and you will be less entan-gled by the manipulative games other people play.

6. I can manage alone

Like the traumatised child in a foetal position, shame, humiliation and powerlessness forces many victims of workplace bullying to curl up in bed or to seek shelter within the walls of their home, far from reality.

Fact

You need regular support from friends at work, your family and personal friends, your chosen health professionals and others to cope and recover. You cannot do it alone.

7. Justice is possible

Like a child, the average adult knows when they are doing something wrong, such as making mistakes, sabotaging teamwork, or being dogmatic, and understand the requirement for consequences. Similarly, they don't realise that when they stand up for their rights, they may exacerbate the bullying games. Thus, when an employee is unfairly mismanaged or bullied, they want an apology or validation as vindication for unfair treatment. When this fails, they seek justice or retribution to prove that they are innocent and did nothing wrong. Most targets believe that financial compensation, no matter how meagre, will justify years of legal action, financial sacrifices and physical and emotional suffering.

Fact

First, common law, equal opportunity and unfair dismissal-type claims to prove your employer's negligence can be very costly and the medico–legal processes may further diminish your psychological wellbeing. Second, a case can take years to get to court. In the meantime it can be extremely difficult to rebuild your life and move on; in other words, you are stuck in time and space. Third, even a million dollar payment obtained via legal proceedings will never compensate for your loss of health and wellbeing. Fourth, if you believe that payouts punish and change organisational cultures, you are wrong, unless it is a very expensive payout linked with heavy negative publicity! So if you take this path remember that justice seldom materialises.

The best solution is to accept that 'shit happens' and move on as soon as possible and resume your life. You may need some healing, and to find new directions and other people or actions to validate you. You need to forgive yourself for being in the wrong place at the wrong time and injured by a toxic workplace. Don't wait for real justice, you will never find it!

However, if there is no other choice, such as when bullying jeopardises your career, then weigh up your options. You can aim for some financial compensation, to exonerate your name and find closure. You can also take some comfort from the fact that bullies don't always get away with it — their health and wellbeing can suffer and they are often forced to leave when they become too expensive to protect. In addition, the knowledge that when your employer is finally made more accountable for your distress, they will be forced make some changes to avoid future payouts, faulty management practices and heavy insurance premiums and this will offer additional validation.

8. It's my way or the highway

You may feel that you have done everything correctly and not done anything wrongly. However, you may be unaware of the times you made others feel incompetent, or jealous, or spoke in an angry tone, or wiggled your finger as though admonishing them.

Fact

There are two sides to every story. Although some employees need to manage a sociopath, most bullies don't mean to abuse you and according to British psychologist Noreen Tehrani (2001) it is hard to separate bullies and targets as they can switch roles, each blaming the other! Some claim that you don't try to socialise, display interest in others or blend in, or that you overreact, or rock the boat over minor or impossible issues. Whatever is occurring, try to find out their version, and what they think and feel about what is happening between you both.

What can a target do?

The moment that you feel that you are being bullied, you need to consider your options and take action. Just like a politician who changes their image from 'ordinary' person to 'public persona' to satisfy the criteria for television screens, you may need to change your facade and discover what will help you survive at work if you decide to remain there.

There are many good ideas in this book and I also encourage you to read *Bully Blocking at Work* (2010) to help you build your survival instinct, empower yourself and obtain professional support. Don't become a whining winger; seek the energy to become a wary warrior and develop your objective evidence. For example, investigate whether your employer, for whom you may have worked so hard, is actually a caring friend or hostile foe. Do they feel responsible for your welfare?

Will they support you the whole way or sabotage you with some form of retaliation once you take action to stop the bullying?

Check out the assertive skills in this book and use them to block them any bullying behaviours before they escalate. Investigate all adversarial and medico–legal systems you may require in the future, to manage them effectively and always obtain feedback from a variety of sources before you take action. And although I encourage you to take a sensible approach, beware that your instincts and need for future progress may mean you want to challenge me and find another path!

What stage are you at?

There are many stages of managing bullying. Each stage may require different skills and strategies in which your therapist can guide you further. They include:

Stage 1: Onset of bullying

Switch on your gut instinct to identify what is happening. Strategy 1 shows you to how to learn to identify and manage your painful feelings, especially your anger and fear. Read Strategy 2 to discover why you are distressed and understand why the events at work are what is actually occurring to you and others. Perhaps you are over-sensitive, over-reacting or misreading the situation, or others are under pressure to obtain profits and don't know how to be better managers?

Imagine that the bullying feels like someone standing on your psychological toes. If this happened, you would tell them to get off as it hurts. Then assess how the bullying behaviours would appear on a video camera. Would it look like you actually being bullied? If it's not bullying, then what could it be?

Stage 2: Take action to block the bullying

Think about your options: Do you confront? (see Strategy 4); Block? (see Strategy 5); Transfer or leave? Obtain help? (Strategy 6); Report? Play a waiting game? Try to pacify the bully? Whatever you do, make sure that you are coping with the strain and releasing painful feelings.

Obtain feedback to make sure that you are not a loose cannon and exacerbating the situation or retaliating, or they may blame you for creating the problem.

Stage 3: Managing the injury

Whether you have been distressed for a brief time or traumatised for many years, you need to maintain your emotional and social resilience. This is where Strategies 1, 2, 3 and 6 are useful. It will also help you to identify and record all the physical, psychological and social symptoms you may have developed that may require assistance or therapy to manage. Below is a list of common signs and symptoms of workplace bullying victims (including all symptoms associated with diagnosing anxiety disorders, depression and post-traumatic stress disorder) not experienced prior to the bullying experience.

Physical symptoms: sleep disorders, nightmares, extreme weight gain or loss, appetite disorders, gastro-intestinal/digestive disorders, cardio-vascular problems (blood pressure problems, angina, palpitations,) severe headaches, sexual difficulties, skin disorders, hair loss, voice changes, asthma, muscular skeletal difficulties (backache, muscle ache, teeth-clenching, jaw pain,) visual difficulties (e.g., blurred vision,) respiratory issues (shortness of breath), facial tics, auto-immune conditions, tinnitus, irregular menstrual cycle, loss of energy/chronic fatigue, suicidality (suicide risk), increased medication, accidents, increased alcohol consumption.

Psychological symptoms: obsessional thinking and reviewing, constant recall of bullying events (especially when lacking validation, hyper-vigilance (paranoia/mistrust), anxiety, irritability, anger, panic attacks, depression, feelings of helplessness/powerlessness, lowered self-esteem and self-confidence, feelings of guilt, failure, humiliation and shame, changes in identity/personality (*'I am different now', 'I am not the same person I was', 'I have changed'*) decreased ability to concentrate or think and speak fluently, mistakes at work, difficult to switch off for any length of time, everything viewed through a 'bullying lens'.

Social symptoms: absenteeism, social avoidance/phobia, (fearful of being near large groups of people), reduced social activities at work, home or with friends, isolation, fear in leaving home, (even going to the letterbox), neglect of normal activities (e.g., housework, gardening, appearance, paperwork,) co-worker resentment, marital tension, parenting difficulties, abandonment by friends outside work, unemployment, inability to manage employment (even in a new job), forced early retirement.

Stage 4: Resolution and self-protection

Eventually the bullying and its aftermath will reduce and traumatic scars will fade. However, you need to mourn your losses and find closure at some stage to move on. Then you will need to insure that this never happens again to you, even in nicer workplaces, and learn the appropriate assertive strategies to block future bullies (Strategies 4 and 5). Then you can feel safe and return to your former workplace or begin working elsewhere.

What do you say to others?

When you become a target of workplace bullying, you will change in some ways. If you are the recipient of minor bullying, followed by immediate validation, protection or removal, the changes will be slight. Alternatively, if you are severely injured you may experience many different personality changes. It is hard to describe the numbing, curdling, internal disintegration or imploding sensations that you may experience. People at work or in your private life may become curious: *'What are you doing? What aren't you working? When will you return to work?'*

Regardless of whether you have signed a confidentiality agreement or not, you need to understand that if you are secretive, due to shame or fear of future legal action by your employer, then no-one can truly support you or understand the evils associated with workplace bullying. Now I am not suggesting that you tell everything to everyone; rather that you obtain psychological and legal assistance to work out what to say to others. For example:

'I have a "toxic employer syndrome" that has affected my ability to fulfil my employment contract.'

'I was injured by management negligence. This has sabotaged my ability to respect them.'

'I have signed a confidentiality agreement with my former employer. Now I suffer psychological, social, cognitive and physical symptoms as a consequence.'

'I can't socialise as much as previously as my adrenaline levels are high, causing a social and public phobia.'

'I am unable to work or clean my house due to my low cortisol levels, caused by workplace bullying trauma.'

'My post-traumatic stress disorder restricts my ability to maintain a normal relationship, please understand.'

The value of therapy and other effective strategies

> 'Even though I am absolutely wacked after a session, I need regular therapy. I don't even know how to describe the difference between my psychiatrist and my psychologist. Both are necessary for me to cope and release some pain, as I can't manage myself as well as I did previously. We discuss similar things but it is different. My psychologist provides a reality check, so while I am in freefall and bounce between reality and fantasy, she brings me back to a stable, safe place where I am respected and validated. I can separate my fears and find new ways of managing myself. It is as though she applies some correction fluid to reduce a few black spots. While I am overloaded with toxic emotions and thoughts, I need to debrief regularly so that I don't explode within the next few days. It's like going through an emotional dialysis unit. Sometimes I ask myself, what did I gain today? The answer is hard to obtain, but I feel better, it is worth the time, travel and exhaustion following the session.'

There are many different areas of your life that can be affected when you are bullied at work. In addition, there are no clear diagnoses for the possible injuries you may suffer and limited evidence-based treatment, besides, the length and variety of medico-legal actions will complicate and exacerbate matters further. Thus you may require a variety of mental health practitioners along your journey to good health and recovery, such as a doctor, psychologist, psychiatrist, as well as others who can help you understand, reduce and manage each symptom eg panic attacks, sleep problems.

Use all the help available

You may require separate professionals for some symptoms — for example, a sleep clinic, anger management course, clinical psychologist for panic attack reduction, psychiatrist for medication; or you may just rely upon your regular counselling psychologist who can help you weather all the storms along the way with supportive therapy, strategic skills training, structural and restorative counselling (see Field, *Bully Blocking at Work*, p. 116). Structural counselling is focused upon helping the client restructure, reprogram or rebuild a totally new life, due to fragmentation of the self or personality change whereas restorative counselling is about restoring what they had — for example, the bullying is like pruning and they can regrow and blossom again without major personality change, but with psychological scarring. Make sure you ask if a psychologist can help you with a particular symptom or can refer you elsewhere. Be aware that the current fixation on popular treatment methods such as cognitive behaviour therapy (CBT) maybe less applicable to long-term trauma (De Vente, Kamphuis, Emmelkamp, & Blonk, 2008), and some excellent generic brands of therapies may have little evidence-based research to demonstrate their effectiveness in treating victims of workplace bullying.

You may also require someone less medical but therapeutic — for example, your minister or spiritual advisor, dietician, gym instructor, masseur, physiotherapist, relaxation/meditation expert, career guidance person, martial arts instructor (to obtain confident body language), naturopath, Feldenkrais expert, or a support group.

Clearly, as understanding, diagnosing and treating targets of workplace bullying is a very new area where few have sufficient knowledge, research or training, you need to need to investigate whom to consult and if necessary, find someone else. Talking to other targets or professional therapists may help you find someone appropriate.

Timeframe

If you consult a therapist early on when the bullying has begun, treatment to manage the bullying and terminate its toxic impact can be quick — around six to eight sessions. It can include information, understanding the causes, professional advice, strategies and skills.

However, if you have been seriously injured, beware that the bullying attacks on all fronts, injuring and destroying many parts of your life and personality, and last for many years. Then you will require long-term counselling, such as fortnightly for six years.

Assessing effectiveness

It is simple to assess short-term treatment because the results establish turning points, leading to instant change, helping you remove, confront or manage the bullying. However, it is much harder to assess if therapy is effective when you are injured over a long period of time.

There are many evidence-based psychological and medical interventions that bring positive therapeutic results, such as hypnotherapy for relaxation, CBT for sleep disorders, anxiety disorders reduction, assertiveness skills and some medications. However, there is a total inadequacy of international, evidence-based treatments for victims of workplace bullying trauma (WBT). Apart from a few European clinics that use a variety of treatment methods for the recently injured, no one has developed the appropriate therapeutic knowledge for assisting the long-term victims of workplace bullying.

Swapping therapists

Remember that there is a belief, especially among the medico–legal fraternity, that you need to stay with the same doctor, psychologist and psychiatrist to demonstrate that you are not a 'doctor shopper' or an unmotivated 'malingerer'. However, they can do more harm than good if you don't feel understood, supported and assisted. Try to discuss any difficulties directly with them, but if you still feel dissatisfied, find someone else.

Take responsibility for your team

> *'Dear Evelyn, with a support group that includes yourself, my GP, my lawyer, Workcover and previous psychologists, I am for the first time able to see a light at the end of the tunnel. I finally feel I will eventually be able to achieve my main goal of returning to work as the confident 'normal' woman I use to be.'*

It may seem a very odd idea, especially when you are feeling desperate, alone and powerless, but you need to build and manage your own support network, comprising professionals (e.g., doctor, psychologist, lawyer) others (e.g., union, case manager), family and friends, as well as a bullying support group (in person or online). This means that like the recovery clinics in Europe, you adopt the role of team leader to do your research, investigate your options and assume ultimate responsibility. Then you can orchestrate any action you wish to take to obtain some validation or justice, improve your health and wellbeing and hasten your recovery. This applies to medication or their alternatives, types of treatment, its frequency and any legal processes you instigate. You can instruct others, provide them with your detailed records, any medical or legal reports, check that they are working in your favour, and coordinate their activities to insure that they are working collaboratively.

Don't allow anyone to tell you what is necessary, effective or advisable. Listen to your gut feelings and assess the unique value of each type of therapy and become responsible for your selection, as you alone know what suits you! You will find that by taking charge, you begin the long journey of resolving painful issues, re-empowering yourself and finding new directions.

Managing your approach to bullying at work

As well as the strategies in this book that will help you move from a state of powerlessness to a state of feeling empowered, following are some general tips that underpin those strategies and provide a useful framework to how you can approach bullying at work.

Score your distress level

Many targets obsess about a few bullying incidents, to the exclusion of all else in their lives. This may magnify the importance of these events, sometimes without regard to reality or their actual significance. It may help to compare each distressful event to other possible stressful life events and estimate their comparative value.

You can begin by estimating everything dreadful that could happen to you on a scale from 1 to 10, where 1 is not very bad and 10 is the worst. For example, losing a loved family member would be 10 out of 10 bad. Developing a life threatening illness? Having a sick child? What about losing the capacity to work anywhere? Losing this job? Losing work friends?

Develop a scale out of 10 of the worst scenarios that could occur and then compare to your current difficulties. How do they compare? Perhaps by using this scale regularly it will help you reduce the amount of emotional spotlight you give to some stresses and help you focus upon more important issues, such as maintaining the rest of your life.

The bullying template

Due to the serious and all-invasive nature of workplace bullying, it tends to create a new, standardised template in your head for managing your world. The template takes over and replaces all previous patterns of behaving, which had been generally successful and productive; due to your heightened vigilance, almost everyone is perceived as bullying when something goes wrong. For example, if you do not receive adequate salary entitlements, it is probably due to administrative error, not bullying. If a mental health professional seems uncaring, it may be caused by their lack of time, understanding or personality, and not a bullying behavior. Thus your role is to constantly compare your perception to reality and get the facts.

Try to recall how you would have handled this type of experience in the past, obtain feedback from your support network about how ordinary people would handle this situation and then adjust your perception and responses to reframe them in order to make them less toxic and more realistic.

Change location

Many painful memories can be associated with a workplace or even your home, once you have been bullied. So you may want to consider making some structural changes to your life, such as changing your job, career or even move home to somewhere with less stressful associations. If this type of move is not feasible, then make some symbolic changes at home — for example, paint your bedroom. You will find that this may act as some form of closure as well as provide some measure of safety, and will be less associated with sad, painful memories.

Reverse cycle of powerlessness

As the bullying increases and your list of managers and bystanders exacerbate the bullying or allow it to fester with neglect, beware that your list of symptoms will grow, extending and oozing out all over your life. Thus, for example, first you avoid the bully, then your colleagues and finally the workplace, or you stop gardening, followed by less housework and grooming, or you see less friends and finally almost no-one.

Clearly, while stuck in a mode of obsessing about what happened, and focusing upon the next step towards gaining some justice, it is hard to maintain or resume normal chores, hobbies, exercise and paperwork, especially when medico–legal difficulties are ongoing.

You need to document your fears and symptoms, and decide what you can do to reduce or bypass them, and what help you require. You could allocate an hour every day on the bullying and related events. Try not to do any more. Simultaneously, don't delay your normal duties due to anxiety; try to manage everyday events, such as doing 10 minutes of paperwork, exercise for 15 minutes, and do a little cleaning every day.

The present, past and future

To avoid becoming totally stuck, obsessed and traumatised within your bullying narrative, you need to build a buffer zone to move in and out, through time and space. Try to spend time thinking about your past (long before the bullying occurred), the present (other things unrelated to the bullying), and your future (when the bullying is over and you have moved on to begin a new life). It may be easier at the beginning to start with *yesterday, today* and *tomorrow*.

Try to imagine a time when this is all over, and you will be left alone by bullies and their cohorts to do other things with your life. This means embedding the word 'hope' more often into your everyday thoughts — for example: *'When this is all over I will …'*, or *'When I am well again, I will …'*, *'Even if I don't get validation or justice I am still alive and can do lots of things with my life'*.

Listen to feedback

There are always options in blocking bullying behaviours, especially before you are severely injured. You may need to speak to many different people, at work and elsewhere — even a five-year-old understands bullying. Many will be able to provide you with another perspective and perhaps even the skills to manage it. Don't judge others and be scared to listen to their viewpoint. It may make the difference you need to manage your situation; the cost of pursuing justice while hurting your family further may no longer seem worth it.

Your employer checklist

Like parents, effective employers realise that bullying can happen anywhere; however, it is up to them to stop bullying so that employees feel safe and respected and can work effectively (Worksafe, 2009). The employer must take ultimate responsibility. In fact, it would be nice if they could thank you for alerting them to any systemic problems which would otherwise interfere with performance, productivity and profits.

- Is your employer collaborative or adversarial?
- Do they validate the perceptions of targets, bullies, and bystanders?
- Do they provide a safe workplace for employees, clients and contractors?
- Do they involve and empower employees in some decision-making regarding their working conditions?

- Do they demonstrate support, respect and understanding to employees?
- Do they update their management practices when there are systemic difficulties; for example, change from annual to quarterly performance reviews, and review exit statements?
- Do they enable non-threatening discussions and constructive confrontations?
- Do they establish effective, fair investigation/restorative practices?
- Do they provide clear explanation of consequences?
- Do they offer regular training/counselling/coaching/mentoring for managers and employees?
- Do they provide rehabilitation, reconciliation, closure, regular audits to prevent future problems?

Your personal resilience checklist

- Record all bullying incidents and positive performance feedback.
- Maintain your physical and emotional health, such as by consulting your general practitioner, a psychologist, psychiatrist, or counsellor. Ensure that you eating properly, exercising and sleeping well.
- Investigate any medication you have been prescribed for evidence it will help your symptoms, or whether there any side effects. Are there non-medical alternatives?
- Consider additional alternative support and assistance — for example, physiotherapy, gym, naturopath, dietician, hairdresser, new clothing, herbal remedies.
- Keep a record of how have you been affected by the bullying, including physical and psychological symptoms, social and economic difficulties, and so on.
- Discover how you can you empower yourself, listen to your gut feelings and take appropriate action to protect yourself.

- Build your social survival skills to obtain support from reasonable people and manage difficult people.
- Improve your communication skills and use courageous chats, constructive or confronting questions when safe to block bullies and handle management.
- Obtain feedback from those you trust to change any of your sabotaging, self-defeating behaviours and learn how to manage others. This includes inquiring whether you have provoked/extended/exacerbated/maintained the conflict in any manner.
- Consider whether you have adequate social support at work and privately or whether you need to improve your support base.
- Try to seek out those with power to help.
- Obtain regular legal and union advice.
- Join a self-help group (online or in person).
- Protect yourself financially as much as possible, without risking your future financial security on risky legal cases.
- Consider your options to distil some public and private validation for yourself.
- Describe your strengths (e.g., writing letters to the media) and weaknesses (e.g., getting angry at the wrong time).
- Consider your options when work is too uncomfortable. For example, can you find another job? Take time off to recover? Find a new direction? Re-train? Move away? Retire?
- Consider what resources are available for you to obtain some measure of justice.
- Decide when you accept that you have had bad luck, that there is no justice and press your restart button to move on.
- Read *Bully Blocking at Work* (Field, 2010) in conjunction with this book.

CHAPTER TWO

Strategy 1: Regulate your feelings

"Josie worked for her family doctor, who sexually harassed and bullied her for a few years until she broke down. She mutilated herself and made numerous suicide attempts. Josie was hospitalised 13 times in 3 years. She couldn't afford to live alone so she was forced to live with her family, including her violent, abusive father. She was filled with rage. Even therapists couldn't cope with her anger and some actually dismissed her. When she came to my office for help, she was angry and aggressive. During early sessions, she needed to express her extreme level of shame, humiliation and powerlessness. As we worked together, she slowly stopped harming herself and began to release her anger in constructive physical ways. She took up karate and, later, indoor soccer, which she described as life savers. Physical activity alone was not enough to release her painful feelings. Sometimes she escaped home by staying with friends in the country. Eventually she moved through her terrible rage and went on to complete her nursing training.**"**

When you are hungry, you eat. When you are thirsty, you drink. When you are angry or afraid, your body is warning you to protect yourself. If you deny your feelings, you paralyse your survival instinct. In this chapter, we learn the first secret of survival in a bullying situation is to recognise and regulate your feelings.

The biochemistry of feelings
Your survival instinct

Every fish, bird or animal (including humans) has a primitive instinct to protect themselves from danger. This survival need is called the fight, flight or freeze instinct. You move into survival mode whenever something you believe is necessary or valuable for your survival is threatened. It may be something minor, like running out of chocolate, or major like being threatened with cancer. It includes your need for financial security and for protecting your good name or your status within your community.

Feelings of being threatened are reflected in your body's biochemical processes. These processes include physical and psychological hormones that control your functioning every moment of the day and help you survive. They form a natural alarm system to warn you about danger and activates your fight, flight or freeze instinct (which we often describe as our gut instinct). Feelings of anger or fear trigger your warning system, which then releases higher levels of stress hormones to energise you to flight or flee. The right amount of hormone helps you to protect yourself by taking constructive action; the wrong amount can overpower, sabotage or paralyse you.

The first step in learning to regulate your feelings is to recognise that emotions like fear and anger are normal, natural and necessary. They warn us of danger and help us to protect ourselves.

Chain reaction

The source of all fear is the amygdala, which is located in your brain. If you become upset, the amygdala is activated and a chain reaction follows. Signals are relayed via the hypothalamus to the adrenal glands, above your kidneys, to pump hormones such as adrenaline and nora-drenaline into your blood. Your breathing, heart rate and blood pressure increase in readiness to take action. More oxygen and glucose is released to provide energy. Your eyes dilate, muscles tense, you feel 'jumpy'; the circulation to your stomach and intestine is reduced and you may feel nauseous. All your senses are heightened and hypersensitive. The pituitary gland sends a message to the adrenal gland to release cortisol and other hormones. They control the body's use of fats, proteins and carbohydrates, place your cognitive functions on alert, recharge your body and even fight disease. All of these changes help prepare you for instant decisions about fighting, running away or playing dead. Once the threat ends, your hormonal system should return to normal.

The impact of trauma

> 'We all experienced the same horror. It's shocking to experience so much betrayal. When you give so much to your job, the social fabric of your life becomes interwoven with that of the job. Ripping it away leaves a profound emptiness and feelings of shame and betrayal. It's a very empty and lonely feeling.'

During a major trauma, your body also shuts down non-essential functions so you have access to more energy to fight or flee. When the trauma ends, some people can move on, thus restoring the hormonal system to normal. Others can't move forward; they're totally absorbed, obsessed or regulated by their traumatic experiences. If you've experienced chronic abuse or trauma, your hormonal system will encounter major difficulties in releasing sufficient cortisol and other hormones to compensate for your earlier losses to restore your body's normal functioning. This is like living in a war zone: you may find it impossible to switch off, so you remain constantly in survival mode.

Post-traumatic stress disorder is essentially a breakdown of your basic survival response. If you believed there was nothing else you could have done — for example, if you were the victim of a hold-up — it is simpler to move on after the trauma. In those cases, you can't blame yourself for being targeted. But in cases of bullying, the target may blame themself at a deep unconscious level for being singled out or not taking the most effective action to block the bullying at the time.

You may wonder why it happened to you, even though you did nothing to deserve it or you were unable to prevent it. Instead of saying *'I did the best I could'*, you may blame yourself and say *'I should have done more.'* You compensate for your perceived lack of action by moving into a continuous state of survival. Your 'delayed reaction' focuses upon fight, flight or freeze. You exist in a state of heightened anxiety, avoidance and anger, trying to do what you believe you should have done before, during and after the trauma. Unlike a broken leg or asthma, trauma can affect nearly everything in your life. Some people remain stuck, paralysed, utterly helpless and unable to move on for years.

Recently, Koren (2010) showed that we can actually determine stress levels after six months by measuring the amount of cortisol level in hair. We know that trauma affects and can injure a number of parts of the brain as Bishop (2011) found that there are two routes in the brain circuitry — that is, the amygdala and ventral prefrontal cortex — which lead to heightened fear or anxiety. Hopefully, it will not be long before future research clearly demonstrates the impact of trauma on all parts of the brain and the body.

Thus trauma can lead to anxiety disorders, post-traumatic stress disorder, panic attacks, depression, damage to your physical health, and even suicide. In fact, recent evidence (Field, 2010; Ferris, 2011) demonstrate that many victims of workplace bullying who can't work demonstrate an identifiable constellation of symptoms, revealing a common profile or pattern of physical, psychological and social symptoms that I have described as workplace bullying trauma (WBT). In my experience, I have found that recovery can be extremely slow for some victims.

Many victims of trauma and abuse, including sexual abuse or domestic violence, and even former prisoners of war can go to work and switch off. They may regard work as a retreat from painful memories. But for victims of workplace bullying, there is no escape from the symptoms of this trauma. It can stalk you everywhere, the agony can be relentless and your fear or horror of anything associated with it is long-lasting. Although your home is your sanctuary, any external reminders, such as a phone call, letter or email, can bring back traumatic flashbacks.

People react to trauma in different ways. Some keep themselves busy all the time, often dealing with medico-legal issues. Others do little, spending most of their day zoned out, in a daze or doing a doona dive. Most spend an obsessive amount of time reviewing what went wrong at work and, subsequently, instead of managing their feelings and moving on, these distressing feelings build up and further injure your mind and body. In other words, the way we respond to trauma can actually make our injuries worse.

EXERCISE

Visualise yourself collecting all your toxic feelings/thoughts/memories and placing them in a box, hidden deep inside you. Sometimes when you are feeling OK you will need to process or release some of these feelings to make more space in the box, otherwise you will burst. At other times you can store them in the box and give yourself room to do something else constructive. The more frequently you release, the greater the likelihood of eventually emptying the box.

A life-changing experience

> 'When I lost my daughter, many years ago, I was deeply trauma-tised. I slowly learned how to cope with the pain; the model of relating I describe in this book grew out of my grief and the things I learned from it. This created the foundation for my first book. When some legal issues meant the book might not be published, my feelings of threat reactivated my original trauma. I changed when I lost my daughter and I changed again when my book was threatened.' Evelyn M. Field

Being bullied can be a devastating experience that arouses conflicting emotions. You need to accept it as a life-altering experience. You will never be the same. When people offer me their stories, years after the experience of bullying, I can see emotional scarring on their faces and in the way they react. Once you identify and confront your feelings about yourself and everyone else involved with the bullying, you can release them constructively instead of internalising them, feeling powerless and becoming paralysed.

Emotional boundaries fluctuate

Under normal circumstances, the average person knows how to deal appropriately with stressful situations. They know when to worry and when to chill out. Sadly, traumatic experiences force you to overreact or show your vulnerabilities. In other words, when you're traumatised, you become stuck in survival mode and can't regulate your feelings. You seem to overreact because you experience emotions more intensely than others. Little things make a huge impact. Instead of a gradual lift or dip of fear or anger, you experience a surge of intense panic or fury. These extreme levels of emotion rise and fall constantly: an off-the-cuff comment, meant as banter, is received with paranoid fear; an official letter signifies doom and gloom. The bullying memories pursue you constantly and affect you emotionally for years.

Slowly, you'll find brief moments where you can cope normally. Eventually, these good periods will increase. As your bad memories fade over time, you can learn how to regulate your feelings and respond appropriately. But, years later, you may still experience the occasional flashback and freeze or over-react.

Why do you need to deal with your feelings?

> *Control your emotions because the person who panics is the one who gets hurt. If you manage your response, you've a better chance of finding a solution. (Shark trainer, Gordon, 2003)*

We know that emotions affect us physically. When fish or cattle are slaughtered in a stressful manner, for example, they release hormones that downgrade the flavour of their flesh. Brain scans of humans show fear, depression, panic attacks, social difficulties and trauma. There is also growing evidence of the impact of stress, anxiety, trauma and anger on the immune system, which increases the likelihood of illnesses such as eczema, ulcers, heart attacks and cancer. Emotions affect every part of your physical, cognitive, social and emotional health. They can sabotage your normal bodily functions and change your ability to think, relate and take action. The evidence is clear and alarming: stress hormones are extremely powerful; fear and anger create bio-chemical havoc.

Explode or implode

If you don't release your emotions appropriately, their toxic impact accumulates. You may tolerate a bad situation for a long time; then something bad happens and you explode. This is known as the 'bottle and burst' method of stress release. You might express your anger by becoming aggressive, like your caveman ancestors (or maybe like your parents).

Alternatively, you may deny your gut instinct and say, 'It will pass'. Then you internalise your anger and stress, which leads to burn-out or breakdown. Either way, you can become stuck, powerless and further traumatised.

When you regulate your feelings, you can empower yourself. You're less likely to remain traumatised and injured if you confront and release your anger and fear. Others are more likely to respect you, understand what's happening and help. When you express your feelings assertively, you access more power to protect yourself; you can confront without provoking, reduce the conflict and block the bully's game. This way you may gain your employer's respect — or empower yourself allow you to separate emotionally and distance yourself from them.

Bullies have feelings too

When I am treating a child who is being bullied at school, I often simplify the situation by saying: 'If you show your fear or anger, you make a bully happy'. Basically, apart from the school's lack of appropriate intervention and lack of parental understanding, the child's emotional reaction actually enables and gives power to the insecure, vulnerable bully to continue their bullying behaviours. Similarly, during a stressful situation at work, most bullies (apart from psychopaths) will feel threatened, and uncomfortable. In other words, when you reveal your fear and anger, whether in an overt or subtle manner, you threaten a bully by mirroring their emotional insecurities. Your behaviours remind them of what they are feeling deep down inside. As they need to protect themselves, they will incorporate their previous experiences and survival instinct to attack you first and, by so doing, inadvertently project their own toxic feelings back onto you.

When you deny your gut feelings, you can't regulate your emotions effectively or identify the toxic feelings that others express and which can injure you, and you may unconsciously prolong the bullying game-conflict. On the other hand, if you express too much emotion, you may frighten others who might help you. If you want to deal with bullies and their cohorts, don't let uncontrolled stress hormones sabotage your survival. The core strategy for dealing with bullying behaviours is to regulate your feelings so that you feel empowered to manage yourself and block others. You need to know when to display, disguise or delay releasing them.

Express or repress

Some cultures are emotionally repressive and believe that identifying and releasing feelings is taboo. Such people pretend emotions don't exist or, if they do, they don't matter. Or they believe that expressing feelings is wrong. Expressions like 'stiff upper lip', 'it's all in the head', 'boys don't cry', 'girls don't get angry' belong to this culture. These people believe suppression and denial will miraculously disintegrate negative feelings.

Although women often share feelings of powerlessness with friends, they don't release their fear or anger; they may internalise and become depressed instead. While most cultures value male aggressiveness, the average man can't express his fear or anger assertively. He may scream at home if he can't scream at work, or run to his cave (or computer) and deny his feelings. This kind of man is more likely to express real emotions when he's drugged or drunk. Sex may also constitute an emotional release for men. It seems that neither gender has developed comprehensive methods for releasing their fear and anger constructively. Both may rely on pharmaceutical or non-medical tranquilisers to release or block their emotional pain.

Sadly, most people confuse the feelings of anger or fear with the faulty method by which they are released. Anger is not bad. It is your survival instinct in action. It must be recognised and released wisely, not repressed. You need to differentiate between constructive ways to release anger, such as the skill of assertiveness, and destructive ways, such as abusing other people.

Don't think of pink elephants

I often ask youngsters how they feel about being bullied. Some say, 'I don't care' but they look upset. So I say, 'Don't think of pink elephants!'

They look surprised. I ask them, 'Well, did you?' That's when I get a smile. 'Yes', they say, 'but just for a moment.' 'Aha', I reply, 'it worked.' When we try to pretend something is not happening, or we don't care about it, it doesn't make it go away. The thought still exists and influences our behaviours.

Most people deny at first that they are being bullied. Eventually they'll acknowledge it, sometimes years later. If you tell yourself you don't care about what the bully does to you, it won't change your real feelings. The bully will instinctively guess you are feeling bad and escalate the bullying behaviours. Even though you may only be experiencing mild bullying, beware of the fact that constant pressure, like water dripping on a stone, inflicts serious physical and psychological damage. Unfortunately, others may realise you are vulnerable but will not help you.

REFLECTIVE MOMENT

Imagine pulling a rubber band as far as it will go. That's how you can feel every day — stressed out and stretched to the limit. Like a rubber band, you'll eventually crack, snap and break — unless you learn constructive ways to release emotion.

What does it feel like?

Rather than pretending it doesn't hurt, it helps to be able to describe your emotions precisely when you are being bullied. Some distressingly common words to describe the way you might feel are: weak, worthless, immobilised, crushed, pathetic, punished, powerless, humiliated, hopeless, rejected, tricked, defamed, devalued, discarded, injured, unsafe, out of control, betrayed, undermined or abandoned.

Some quotes from the targets of bullying on how they feel

'I felt unreal, surreal. It was a Molotov cocktail of bad feelings.'
'I could see the shark fin in the water. I was being circled.'
'Four incidents were so frightening I could have died on the spot.'
'I was orchestrated out. It felt like a rape.'
'It was soul destroying. I didn't deserve this. I did nothing wrong.'
'It's like Chinese water torture.'
'I felt frozen in time, marginalised, minimised, ostracised.'
'I felt like a schoolboy being yelled at in public.'
'Because it was a group, I felt more threatened and fearful.'
'I felt like a suffragette, complaining about the bullying.'
'I was hauled over the coals. I became a blubbering mess.'
'I kept hoping they'd care about me.'
'I became sick before work in the morning. It was psychic terror.'
'I was a ticking time-bomb waiting to explode. My life was on hold.'
'Since I've been bullied for the third time, I feel like a bully magnet.'
'I hate it when they say, "Pull yourself together".'
'My identity has gone, I feel like a nothing at work since the bullying began.'
'I felt trapped, like a prisoner on day leave.'
'I can't get it out of my head.'
'I felt like my personality had been killed. I was afraid to be me.'
'I used a razor blade to cut my arms. Instead of feeling numb, I can feel myself.'
'There's no evidence but I know what they did to me.'

Part 2: Managing your feelings

Living with trauma

A concert of traditional Jewish songs was held in the beautiful old Spigeltent in Melbourne. Author Arnold Zable acknowledged some elderly people in the audience. He mentioned that they had sung these songs in concentration camps during WWII.

Being the victim of workplace bullying can feel like a living hell but it does not compare with incarceration in one of Hitler's concentration camps. Yet, even in concentration camps, people survived by doing creative things to help detach themselves from their horrific lives. They could not control their chances of physical survival, but they could manage their belief systems; however, they needed to release some of their emotional pain to keep their sanity and maintain their desire to survive. If it is possible to find ways to release toxic feelings in a concentration camp, it is possible for you too.

REFLECTIVE MOMENT

Sit in a quiet place and make yourself comfortable. Become aware of the variety of painful, distressing feelings you've been experiencing. If you're feeling stuck, remember to look for any fragment of anger, fear and sadness. Then work out how to release them from your body or record them in your personal diary. Consider the following points:

- Are your feelings affected by past or current stresses?
- Do they bring back memories of earlier abuse or bullying?
- Write down nasty memories, or flashbacks, that loiter in your mind.
- Are you frightened of more abuse?
- Are you feeling angry but powerless?
- How do you feel about the bully, workmates and managers, especially those who have been unhelpful or who have hindered, betrayed or sabotaged you?
- How do you feel about who is helping and what's been done to help you survive?
- What concerns do you have about the future?

Re-label your experience

Whenever Josie mentioned her bully, her voice reverberated with fury and hatred. She found it difficult to pronounce his name and stumbled over the letters. I suggested we re-label him — she called him 'pigface' for years.

It's less painful to use new labels to describe your bully and your experiences. It may bring a smile to your face and empower you. Look for different labels and encourage your friends and family to use them too. Here are some examples of re-labelling from my clients:

The bullies

'I didn't see weasel face today.'
'How's the shark? Still in a feeding frenzy?'
'She's a real fruitcake.'
'He smells like rotten meat.'
'Comparing my old boss to my new one is like comparing nashi pears to prickly pears.'
'She's a bulldozer.'
'The snake bites when threatened.'
'She weaves a spider's web.'
'He belongs to the BWC (Big Wankers' Club) species.'

The experience

'... trapped on a limb'
'... paralysed like a deer in front of headlights'
'... on a roller coaster ride'
'... caught in a mouse trap'
'... works like a maze. I went in and got lost.'

The workplace

'... full of pirahnas'
'... the old boy's club'
'... it's dog eat dog'
'I'm in a wasp's nest'
'They keep moving the goal posts.'
'... glad I've left the minefield.'

Understand power

Although you feel powerless when you are being bullied, the way you express your feelings makes a difference to the power you have. There are three ways of expressing power: passively, aggressively or assertively and one way is more powerful than the others.

Passive

You lose power when you express your feelings passively.

> *Jillian was very upset when she wasn't invited to the staff party by email. She cried in the toilet and took a day off, but she didn't tell anyone.*
>
> *Fred was silent at work but yelled at home. He took lots of sick days and left the job without giving anyone feedback.*

If you express or release your feelings passively, it is difficult to decipher exactly what you're feeling. Your true feelings are disguised behind a façade. You may internalise your emotional pain and develop a multitude of physical, psychological and social symptoms. On the other hand, if you complain to someone without authority or explode, you are being passive aggressive and your behaviour may frustrate others who find it difficult to understand, empathise and help you.

Aggressive

You abuse power when you express your feelings aggressively.

> *Brendan often yelled at the office girls to stop chatting and work. They were angry but they didn't bother with internal grievance procedures and went straight to a lawyer.*
>
> *The moment bullying was reported, Human Resources instigated a formal investigation, instead of chatting to staff to find out what was really going on.*
>
> *Bob was angry that his lies were discovered. He closed the door and yelled for two hours: 'You fucking woman, I told you what to do.'*

If you suddenly explode, screaming and abusing others, it's as though you are vomiting your emotions all over them. The toddler tantrum doesn't build respect at work, but you're probably oblivious to the damage you've caused. Generally, people aren't sympathetic to people who are overly dramatic, aggressive and lacking respect for others. Paradoxically, you won't obtain much relief from your performance so you may internalise remaining anger and become ill.

Assertive

We use our power when we express our feelings assertively.

> 'I feel upset when you yell at me and I can't work,' Joy said to her manager. He stopped.
>
> 'I'm annoyed with the looks and snide comments from the boys' cycle club,' Jill told her manager. She was transferred to another section.
>
> 'I value constructive feedback but I'm unaware of any reason for your criticism. Please show me evidence.'

You behave assertively when you identify your feelings and release them non-verbally or when you express them directly in a quiet, firm, non-aggressive manner. This shows that you're taking responsibility for what you say and is less threatening because you are not attacking them – you're just expressing yourself. This can make it very hard for them to continue and escalate the bullying game. You will also feel better for releasing some painful feelings.

There is a bonus for behaving assertively. Magically, you make the bully accountable to you and you receive instantaneous feedback which demonstrates whether or not they care about you. You need this feedback to plan your next step.

> You to bully: 'I'm upset that I wasn't included in the project. It's part of my role description.'
>
> Response: 'So what?'
>
> You: 'Thanks for the feedback.'

It is, indeed, valuable feedback. If they don't care, you can set about protecting yourself. Eventually you'll question why you're working so hard for an employer or manager who doesn't care about you. That's when you'll prepare to take your next step.

Consider this alternative response:

> You: 'I'm upset that I wasn't included in the project. It's part of my role description.'
>
> Response: 'I understand that you're upset but you and the team aren't collaborating well.'
>
> You: 'What can we do to improve the situation?'

If they do care, they'll respect your feelings, listen to your feedback and try to resolve the situation. Another bonus of this approach is that assertive people are generally liked, trusted and respected.

Feedback and power

You can lose, abuse or use your power, depending on whether you choose passive, aggressive or assertive responses. If you use your power assertively, the worst that can happen is that you get valuable feedback, which helps you plan your next step. At best, you win respect and liking and find a way to resolve the situation.

Regulate your feelings

When you need to eat, drink or go to the toilet, you don't question or deny — you take action instinctively. You need to treat your feelings and emotions, especially anger and fear, like any other instinct. They are warning you of danger. Once you identify the warning signals, you can take action to protect yourself. If you deny your feelings, you paralyse your survival instinct and can't protect yourself. If you express too much emotion, you frighten others and empower the bully. Then your situation can become unbearable and you can break down.

When you acknowledge your feelings and release them appropriately, you are more likely to regain your power. You can compare this to letting off steam, not like a geyser, which explodes, but like a pot simmering on the stove. Alternatively, imagine this is your emotional disposal unit, emotional dialysis, or just a way to maintain your emotional elasticity. When you regulate your feelings, it's like using a sensor light to confront danger and a dimmer switch to lower the intensity. My concept of regulation of feelings was published in my book *Bully Busting* (1999) while Davidson's (2009) research using brain-imaging techniques, shows that the brain is not a fixed entity, thus emotional regulation changes in response to experience and training.

You regulate your feelings by:

- identifying them
- quantifying them
- releasing them in constructive, assertive ways.

If it's difficult to be assertive at work, then release your feelings in less risky ways. See page 45 for ideas on releasing your feelings.

The main feelings to regulate

We have four basic feelings: happiness, sadness, anger and fear. Happiness and contentment is your eventual goal, your guide to feeling safe, although you won't experience this during the bullying. Sadness follows the release of anger and fear and is associated with loss, mourning and depression. So when bullying ends, you'll experience sadness; it is a necessary stage for moving on. Generally, bullies don't get any reaction from sad or happy people. Ultimately, your anger and fear are the main feelings to regulate — in other words, your fight or flight instinct. Sometimes it's hard to identify the core feeling, so let's explore a variety of words that might be meaningful to you.

Happiness: comfort, contentment, gladness, cheerfulness, calm, peace, delight, pleasure, bliss, enjoyment, elation, glee, exhilaration, ecstasy.

Sadness: depression, misery, feeling down, mourning, grief, gloom, despondency, dejection, sorrow, unhappiness, wretchedness, desolation, woe.

Anger: irritation, indignation, antagonism, resentment, frustration, aggravation, being cheesed or pissed off, annoyance, provocation, fury, fuming, madness, frenzy, rage, being upset or incensed or livid.

Fear: concern, edginess, being uneasy or baffled, apprehension, uptightness, confusion, exasperation, panic, pressure, being afraid or stressed, nervousness, tension, anxiety, worry, fright, fright, terror.

Action: follow these steps to regulate your feelings

You need to identify, quantify and release your feelings to empower yourself. Although this program might appear simple, it can help anyone, including severely traumatised people. Here's how you do it.

1. Identify

It's simple for most people to identify physical sensations like hunger, tiredness or thirst. It's more complicated to identify core emotional feeling, such as anger, fear and sadness, or complex feelings such as fury, disbelief, terror, shame, powerlessness, humiliation, disgust, rage, mourning or devastation.

Check every part of your body to see if you're affected. If you're feeling angry, you may frown constantly, clench your hands and grit your teeth at night. If you're forced to see the bully, you may experience fear in the form of nausea, sweaty palms, or perspiration, or you may find you are jiggling your arms and legs. If you're dreading a meeting or opening an email, you may have a panic attack. Sometimes you may be unaware of the emotion but find you are eating or drinking more than usual, have difficulty concentrating or experiencing more headaches, stomachaches or sleep difficulties. You'll probably experience combinations of feelings, such as embarrassment (fear) and shame (anger) while talking to friends.

Action — Ask yourself:

What am I feeling right now?

What did I feel when … happened?

What is the other person (bully, bystander, manager, friend family member) feeling when I …

2. Quantify

The amount of hunger or thirst you feel can vary. Likewise, you need to quantify your feelings to work out how much to release, how often, and how and when to do it. This reduces the build-up of toxic emotion inside of you, reduces the severity of panic attacks, and improves your overall functioning and relationships.

You need to estimate, on a scale of 1 to 10, the quantity of each feeling. You should do this five times a day, seven days a week. You can plot your feelings on a chart to obtain an average. An anger score of 3 out of 10 isn't high, whereas an anger score of 9 out of 10 influences everything you do. The higher your score, the more frequently you'll need to monitor and release.

If you're extremely distressed, release three to five times a day. If you're overwhelmed with anger and fear, release every 90 minutes. As your situation improves and you have less emotional pain to release, reduce the frequency. When you feel better, you may release frustrations once a week by playing sport, movies or yoga, the way most people do.

Action — Ask yourself:

How much am I feeling right now on a scale of 1 to 10?

3. Release

Every day, you make decisions about what to eat and drink, when and where. You decide according to your appetite, your mood, the time of day, your location and your companions. In the same way, you need to decide how to release your anger, fear and sadness as everyone reacts differently to anxiety, depression and trauma. There are many techniques for releasing feelings that are influenced by the time available, your work location and your home.

Look for activities that release each feeling. For example, meditation or dark chocolate may release anxiety. Physical exercise, gardening or chopping up a pumpkin for pumpkin soup may release anger. Humour and exercise release most feelings. Some people prefer to be busy; others need to mull things over. You may feel relieved when you play with your dog or take a long walk. It doesn't matter what you do, even if it is just a placebo (Lieberman, Jarcho, Berman, Naliboff, & Suyenobu, 2004) so long as it reduces negative stressful feelings. Find out what works for you, write it down and, when you're feeling bad, use your options.

Action — Ask yourself:

What am I going to do now to release my feelings?

4. Four types of release:

There are four simple types of release: verbal, physical, direct and indirect.

You may like to write down a number of activities so that when you're feeling bad, you know what to do. Here are some examples of different release activities. By trying them, or from previous experience, you will learn which ones suit you.

Verbal direct: Tell the bully how you feel about what he is doing to you, when it is safe to do so. Beware that it may not work with a serial bully, who doesn't want to respect you.

> *'I feel frustrated when you withhold information that is vital to my work.'*
> *'I feel angry that you always ridicule me.'*
> *'I'm confused. I don't understand why you need to intimidate me.'*

'I think you're frustrated with me. Can you tell me why?'

'I'm deeply distressed by your behaviour towards me right now. I need a break and will discuss this with you later on.'

Verbal indirect: Inform your contact officer, line manager or another worker that you are upset at the bully's behaviour and ask for assistance, provided that your career will not be endangered. Record your request in your diary.

Physical direct: Punch a punching bag, throw gravel or ice at a wall, open macadamia nuts, squeeze bubble wrap, exercise, play stress ball or any kind of ball game, throw darts at the bully's photo, burn an effigy, smash a dough doll or one made of calico.

Physical indirect: Watch a funny TV show, dig in the garden, use a warm scented facecloth, light incense or have a massage. Use Bach herbal remedies. Try some kind of physical relaxation like yoga, Tai Chi, Feldenkrais, Alexander technique, Pilates, Shiatsu or Reiki. Ask your family or friends to cuddle you, hug a favourite teddy bear or a tree. Maybe you enjoy bubble baths or scented shampoo.

You may want to change your habits or environment in case they bring back painful memories. Try changing your home décor or your hairstyle or taking up different hobbies. Alternatively, you may need to develop regular habits or rituals like listening to music, reading a magazine, going for a drink or writing your diary. Design a 'chill-out' list of activities that you can do when you find yourself over-obsessing

about the bullying — for example, baking biscuits, window shopping or taking an overnight holiday. Don't despise TV, computers and electronic games — they give some people a temporary break. Others will choose objects that provide an anchor for peace and optimism, like a religious symbol or a special key chain. And seek help, including professional help — don't end up piggybacking other stresses onto the pain you feel from being bullied.

For people who enjoy structure, a timetable for identifying, quantifying and releasing, like the one below, may be helpful. Remember to include each stressful feeling:

Time of day	Mon	Tues	Wed	Thur	Fri	Sat	Sun
Morning	Walk with a friend	Meditate	Surf the net	Walk with my dog	Meditate	Swim	Walk
Mid-morning	Tea/coffee	Windowshop				Yoga	
Lunch	Talk with friends			Tasty lunch		Garden	Read
Afternoon	3 mins of visualisation	TV	Deep breathing			Hobby	TV
Evening	Bubble bath	Punch a bag	Chocolate	TV	Meet a friend	Movies	Try new recipe

Recharge your mind

Many people can release their feelings with mental exercises like the ones below. See if any of these are helpful for you.

1. Feeling meditation: This helps to release painful memories you have stored. Find a restful spot and close your eyes. Imagine that your four main feelings are colours. For example, happiness might be yellow; sadness, blue; anger, red and fear, orange. Now travel through your body, looking for where you find the different colours. When you find a painful feeling, identify it, breathe into it, stay with it and then, when you are ready, let it go.

2. Mental relaxation: The idea of this is simply to feel still and quiet inside and release painful feelings for a little while, which can energise you to fight future battles. Try 10 to 20 minutes of relaxation or meditation a day. This could include deep breathing or just thinking about something or someone that makes you feel good. If you don't know how to meditate, it could be worth finding a teacher or a book to help you learn a simple technique. And don't forget the benefit to some people of going to a church, synagogue, mosque or ashram to meditate and pray.

3. Humour: Humour is used in hospitals to help people recover and in factories to reduce stress. It stimulates your immune system, promotes healing and relaxation and reduces negative feelings. Humour provides a different perspective. It's a healthy way to hit back at authority, especially when you're feeling powerless. It can make you feel normal, when bullying at work has made you feel you're not. It triggers positive feelings, like hope and optimism. You can't be anxious or angry and laugh at the same time. There are numerous downtrodden, persecuted cultures, like the Jews or the Irish, that use humour as a survival mechanism. You can go to funny movies, use funny expressions or laugh at yourself. Some people found these lines funny:

> Jewish telegram: Start worrying. Details to follow.
>
> I'm not tense, just terribly, terribly alert.
>
> My girlfriend asked if I slept well. I said no, I made a couple of mistakes.

Bodywork

As well as the physical direct and indirect release techniques described on pages 45 to 47, the following techniques provide release and ease for some people.

Healing sounds: Some people relax when they hear the sounds of nature, such as birds singing or running water. You may find soft music is calming and loud music releases anger. Others need to make their own noises to release pain — whistling, singing or grunting, for example. You could try screaming into a cushion or in the car when nobody's around. Even barking like a dog could help. It uses the diaphragm and releases stress. Maybe it will even make you laugh. I know people who get release from swearing in different languages or making up their own words. Others find relief by sounding out the words they feel, slowly, emphasising and stressing each letter at a time. Aaa ... Nnn ... Ggg ... Rrr... Yyy — angry, then try words like 'ashamed', 'humiliated', 'furious'.

Healing sights: Some people feel better when they look at lovely things. You could browse through a book or your collections, go to a film, a gallery or a museum, walk in a forest or by the beach. Retail therapy needn't be expensive. Go to a market, a garage sale or an auction and buy something nice and cheap, go window shopping in an elegant shopping centre.

Healing scents: Scent is very powerful. It remains imprinted in your mind long after other memories go. You may try a new perfume or after-shave or be comforted by the scents of a newly mown grass, fresh bread, coffee, home cooking, an open fire, fresh flowers or an oven roast.

Healing food: From childhood, we all associate food with emotional comfort. Although you need a healthy diet, comfort foods in moderation can help you feel better. Maybe you would like schnitzels, potato chips or icecream occasionally? Certain liquids are famous for the comfort they bring: chicken soup, for example, or herbal tea, or a small amount of your favourite alcoholic drink, such as beer, Baileys, brandy or Dom Benedictine.

Here are some ways that some of my clients have chosen to regulate their feelings:

- Bill runs every day and takes a shower when he's angry.
- Maria likes a glass of wine, incense, soft candles and music.
- Rena enjoys travel: 'It helps me use a different part of my brain'.
- Mary cleans up her garden and plants vegetables.
- Scott's quick wit and humour provides him with positive feedback, which compensates for the damage caused by the bullying.
- Lena reminds herself to breathe and goes to the beach.
- Helen recorded the number of times she stressed about the bully in one hour. She calculated he wasn't worth the investment.

Strategy 1 in brief

Emotions like fear and anger are helpful in warning you of danger. Don't ignore them, but don't express them unwisely either. Learn techniques of assertiveness, rather than of aggression or passivity. To prevent long-term injury to yourself and others you need to learn how to regulate your feelings. That involves identifying your feelings, quantifying them and finding release techniques that work for you. You have the power to help yourself.

CHAPTER THREE

Strategy 2:
Understand the reasons

❝I had the best of worlds: a good family, a lovely home and an exciting career as a primary school headmistress. I ran the school like clockwork and implemented an anti-bullying program. For five years, everyone respected and praised me. Just after I obtained government registration for the school, there was bullying, malicious rumours and death threats against me. My staff became disrespectful, outspoken and militant and my sister witnessed staff plotting to get rid of me. At first, I couldn't understand why. The school's principal gave mixed messages and I naively believed he would support me. I didn't protect myself and forgot that I'd been warned about his regular betrayal of staff. I felt as though I'd been raped. Slowly I realised that the bullying had nothing to do with me. The local grapevine gossip filtered through. At first, it seemed to come from the principal's jealous wife, but the real instigator was the school board. They resented my association with the senior church. Following the school's registration, they manipulated the principal's wife to create a gang to bully me out. Staff were cajoled into betraying me. I was a football kicked between the school and senior church officials. **❞**

Why is your search for reasons important?

Most people aren't born to be either a bully or a target for bullying. A small percentage of the population has an anti-social personality disorder, but most bullies are simply ignorant, insensitive copycats, or poorly managed managers who feel themselves to be under attack (Wood, 2009, personal communication). And, apart from a small percentage of extremely sensitive people, most targets are ordinary people in stressful, powerless and traumatic situations.

Understanding the reasons you are being bullied is empowering. It is your path to survival, allowing you to assess the impact, find out what you can do to help yourself, obtain the support you need and move on. It is worthwhile to try to find out what factors were operating to make you a target for bullying or a bully and to assess your employer. Alternatively, you can regard it as one of life's misfortunes, as a challenge sent by the universe to inspire you to improve the rest of your life or nudge you to helping others. Probably a train of events occurred over a period of time to increase the likelihood of you becoming a target or a bully or both. Don't blame yourself for not being superhuman.

Understand yourself

If you've been conditioned during childhood to blame yourself for things that go wrong, you can remain stuck in the role of victim, never learning to protect yourself. Alternatively, if you've never experienced difficult, nasty people before, you'll blame the bully, his mob and disloyal colleagues, without fully understanding the situation. You need to understand the reasons for their behaviours and your own behaviours and to accept that your employer has also abused his legal, ethical and financial responsibilities. When you understand more fully, you can change the cycle of anger, fear, defensiveness and powerlessness. Once you understand why you were bullied, victimised and injured, you're less likely to feel ashamed.

Factors from your childhood

'I was different to the other school students. My siblings and parents were older, so I was more mature. My asthma kept me inside at lunchtime, while other students played outside in the freezing Scandinavian winter. I was bullied until my parents confronted the school. Later on, I did my MBA in the United States. I travelled the world as a highly paid executive. I can make fair, tough business decisions and place high demands on my staff. But my management style is gentle, firm and consultative. I'm a collaborative team player, not a macho, aggressive type.

> *'Unfortunately, my management style is regarded as wimpy and non-aggressive in Australia. I've had three nasty workplace bullying experiences and been subjected to the same tactics I experienced at school. In 23 years and 19 managers, I've had three bullies. One employer sent me to the head office in the United States and I was extremely successful. Their other golden boy was Bill, a senior executive, who'd gone to the United States a few years earlier. When I returned home, I discovered that every new idea I submitted was torn to shreds and rejected by Bill. After numerous rejections, my immediate supervisor, Fred, realised his game. We submitted my ideas under Fred's name. Bill said they were excellent; he wasn't threatened because he thought they came from Fred. When I resigned, Bill went berserk and revealed his true colours. He said, "You're a useless piece of shit; this saves us a problem. You'll regret this for this rest of your life."'*

The foundations of resilience, assertiveness or vulnerability begin in childhood. There are many reasons why children become targets of school bullying, although not all will be bullied at work. A full discussion of this is presented in my book *Bully Blocking* (Field, 2007) but here are some of the childhood factors that may have affected you:

- You were bullied by nasty students in a school with incompetent teachers and irresponsible management.

- You became powerless because school bullying was a minor issue compared to family difficulties, especially around puberty.

- You experienced other traumas as a child, but your parents couldn't protect you because of their own difficulties.

- Perhaps one or both parents were over-controlling or abusive. You couldn't challenge their values and rules. If you couldn't say no to a parent who loved you, it would be even harder to say no to those who don't care about you.

- You always tried to please a parent, so they would appreciate and love you. They never expressed it but you kept on trying.

- You were a special child, over-protected by doting parents and became accustomed to everyone treating you with respect but without the acuity to be wary and protect yourself when dealing with mean or manipulative strangers.

- You didn't have practice dealing with difficult people, because nobody argued or challenged one another at home.
- You were shy or sensitive, or you experienced social or personality difficulties.
- You were different. For example, you were gifted, handicapped or culturally different and you felt inferior.
- You always had a strong belief in standing up for justice and challenging unethical or unproductive behaviours, thereby threatening corrupt bullies and inept managers; for example, by stating: *'This isn't fair; I did nothing wrong; why should I be bullied?'* or *'At my last job there was a far better way to do this.'*

What blocked your survival instinct?

Everyone is born with a survival instinct — the primitive ability to sense danger and protect yourself in the wild or the work jungle. As you have seen in Strategy 1, your gut feeling or fight/flight instinct is normal, natural and necessary and provides you with the biochemical energy to take action. Thus, when you confront danger, you switch on your survival instinct.

Some people identify the bullying but underestimate its impact, so although you were aware and may have had a choice to leave or manage it differently, you did not realise how bad it would become.

But what happens if the danger is invisible, subtle or has infiltrated everywhere? Bullying at work can be hard to acknowledge, measure or prove. Then your conscious mind doesn't pressure you to take action. Perhaps something in your past trained you to switch off when you should have been more alert. Maybe you didn't trust your survival instinct, so you couldn't absorb what was actually happening, thereby becoming increasingly stuck, helpless, vulnerable and unprotected and consequently open to further bullying.

Many people learn to keep secrets from themselves. Thus you deny your thoughts and feelings, ignore your vulnerabilities, overestimate your strengths, and underestimate the bully's toxic power or your manager's support. Alternatively, people keep secrets from you that might explain why you were targeted, such as the fact the bully needs to hide his mistakes or find a cheap way to reduce his staff numbers.

If you've experienced an earlier trauma, and even though bullying constitutes a very different trauma, the new threat can paralyse you like a rabbit in front of headlights. Victims of violence survive by using defence mechanisms such as disassociation (distancing yourself) or sublimating (focusing on your work) to survive. These defence mechanisms create blind spots that stop you identifying danger and protecting yourself. Also, if you have an increased sensitivity to trauma, your body produces less cortisol to fuel your survival. You become further stuck and powerless. Once you discover what's blocking your survival instinct, you can treat it like a computer virus that requires reprogramming. Then you can acknowledge the bullying that is occurring, activate your survival instinct and protect yourself.

You didn't use your survival instinct if you:

- didn't listen to your gut feelings
- believed the bully was a teddy bear, not a brown bear
- pretended your boss was normal, not arrogant, abrasive or ambitious (see Crawshaw, 2007)
- loved your job and didn't want to leave
- worked harder to please the bully and combat their criticisms
- didn't confront the bully about their behaviours in a rational, respectful manner
- didn't acknowledge your right to protect yourself
- reported the bullying and, when no one took action, you waited in vain
- hid your distress from managers who may have taken action
- waited until bullying escalated, making it too late for simple interventions
- believed your organisation operated with respect and justice, not betrayal, when the facts were different and others had also been bullied
- believed your employers cared about you, oblivious to the evidence that they didn't.

Earlier vulnerabilities

> *'My upbringing turned me into a goody-goody. When I was in Grade 5, the principal took me outside and spoke to me in full view of the class. I didn't have a new Bible. It cost five pounds, which my family didn't have. It was a minor event, but it affected me deeply. Since then, I always carry a sense of shame and humiliation. It affects me wherever I am. Automatically, I feel others deserve more and it always makes me feel excluded, second-best and second-hand.'*

Some people carry painful scars of powerlessness, humiliation and poorly designed coping strategies from childhood through adolescence into their workplaces. Like cracks in a bridge, these scars lie there dormant, waiting for a stressful situation to surface. Thus, for example, if you had difficulties managing your father and stepfather simultaneously, you could project these difficulties onto juggling your two current but very different bosses. Alternatively, you coped by turning a blind eye to your abusive family, but expected everyone else to be nice and caring; unlike ordinary people who recognise that all types go to work! The damage is latent and can create a cumulative effect. It can cloud your ability to identify potential dangers. When you ignore, you disempower yourself.

Were you squashed while growing up?

> *Effie grew up in an abusive family and accepted bullying as normal. She tolerated her bully boss for a long time.*
>
> *Mary's parents had so many problems, she couldn't confront them about little things. She became powerless. When bullied, she automatically went into victim mode. This was an invitation to the bully to keep attacking.*
>
> *Bella was bullied by her father, a stern, controlling minister. She then married a criminal sociopath, who also bullied her. Later on, she was bullied out of her high profile career.*

The late Anita Roddick, founder of the 'Body Shop' chain stores, believed that her determination to succeed stemmed from never having been squashed by her parents. From early on, she was allowed to initiate many new ideas and challenge preconceived ways of doing business.

EXERCISE

Sit down alone, or with a caring person. Can you identify your original bully, the first person to make you feel powerless? Then name others who squashed you. How did these experiences affect you? Perhaps you recall others who empowered you? What skills do you need to develop to stop being bullied?

Some current factors

Wrong place, wrong time

> The first thing that strikes you about Sharon is her warm, wonderful smile and intelligent eyes. She is attractive, assertive and capable. She has excellent social skills and a supportive family. At one stage, she worked for a sociopathic bully. Despite the safe passage of time, she looked very upset when she described her bullying experience with him. Then it struck me very clearly. If someone like Sharon can be bullied, it can happen to anyone.

Although being the victim of a hold-up is a distressing, traumatic experience, a target doesn't blame themselves. They just accept that it was bad luck. In contrast, targets of bullying often say: *'I can't believe what's happening to me'* or *'I can't understand why they're bullying me'.* However, it may be that you're just in the wrong place at the wrong time. In fact, there is no clear clinical evidence that links your personality before the bullying to an increased likelihood of being a target. Anyone can be a bully or target, including nice, successful, intelligent, assertive men and women in any career. According to Djurkovic, McCormack and Casimir (2006) bullying, rather than having a neurotic predisposition, is the major contributor to negative impact and therefore to the physical symptoms in a victim. Being an employee in a dysfunctional organisation is like being in the centre of a dartboard. Sooner or later, someone will throw a dart at you. Despite your personal strengths, many other factors can block your ability to protect yourself.

Don't blame yourself

Camellia trees have beautiful flowers, but they won't grow in the tropics because they require a temperate climate. Don't blame yourself for being in the wrong place at the wrong time. You would have been fine somewhere else. Hopefully you will plant yourself somewhere else later on that suits your temperament.

My daughter can't eat anything with monosodium glutamate as she could have an allergic reaction and collapse. Thus some factors can make you more vulnerable — for example, gender, or the economic climate. Similarly, people have died in bushfires trying to save their animals or family photos. Although you should have fled the bullying at the time, you thought you were doing what was right.

Being nice is not always nice

> Sue has been a highly respected politician for years. 'How do you handle the bullies in politics?' I asked her. 'I grew up with three older brothers and can yell back myself. Plus, I learned how to handle a bullying grandfather,' she replied.

I often meet parents who encourage their children to be nice to others: *'If you're nice to others, they'll be nice to you'.* This is theoretically sound but doesn't always work in practice. Children confuse being nice with being vulnerable. School bullies can regard 'nice' children as easy targets.

Likewise, the nice adult believes in respect, empathy and teamwork. They have been brought up to believe that if you're nice others will be nice and if something goes wrong, they'll receive justice according to the stated policies. While they may appear to be collaborative, bullies are competitive and adversarial. They view some employees as suckers to be used and abused.

Being different

> Claudia was a Gen Y woman. She was ambitious and outspoken. She threatened the older male dinosaurs at work, who ganged up against her.

Unless they've learned tolerance, most people are threatened by someone who is different. This includes differences of age, gender, religion, ethnicity, nationality or physical deformities, as well as people who don't belong to the main social group, have too many fancy holidays, are too intellectual or too conscientious. Australian Aboriginals regard eye contact as disrespectful. Their manager bullies them when he says: 'Look at me when I talk to you'. They are accused of going walkabout when they leave the office to go to another department. The hearing impaired person is denigrated for not hearing, or for only hearing when they want to. Homosexual, bisexual or transgender people constantly confront subtle and overt forms of homophobic bullying. Some people discriminate against their own race when their skin shade is different. Although many parliamentarians and political advisers are over 60, people of that age in the workforce are seen as suitable fodder for retirement villages, not as worthwhile employees. If you're regarded as different, you can be alienated and bullied out.

Quiet achievers

These employees are conscientious, generally well liked and competent. If you have a strong value system about your work and believe your employer values your contribution, you can forget that everyone is replaceable. Perhaps everything was fine for years, and then changes occurred, such as a takeover, new manager or a shift in company values. Maybe you were naive or oblivious to altered office politics. When the bullying begins, you try to correct any hint of unprofessional conduct, without realising you're playing into their trap. You work harder, but the bullying doesn't go away.

Unfortunately, competent, conscientious targets threaten incompetent bullies, their passive co-workers, inept managers, and their slack employees. They sabotage and undermine quiet achievers in an attempt to build their own profile. These bullies are foolish because, if they valued the competent employees, they would work even harder and increase their own success, but it is no use hoping that managers will stop being so stupid and self-sabotaging.

The provocateur

Some employees get very frustrated when things go wrong. They know the bully has no right to use unfair, disrespectful, unethical behaviours so they challenge, expose wrongdoings and refuse to join the bully clique. Their anger can inflame others. If this is your situation, you may need to reconsider. Although you may be correct, it doesn't always pay off. While you fight for justice instead of finding safer and more suitable options, you can inadvertently escalate a conflict and unwittingly reward the bully.

The stress will affect your work and irritate other employees and your employer. The battle will continue unrelentingly until you can't cope. Unlike a domestic quarrel, where some form of compromise or resolution is necessary for peace, there's no such expectation at work. Your confrontation challenges the status quo and some will bounce back and attack you.

The vulnerable person

This employee is often conventional, conscientious, compulsive and less socially sophisticated. If you are sensitive, anxious, with low self-esteem or you interpret every tease or criticism as an attack, then your inner bully reinforces these negative messages. Your vulnerability lowers your tolerance level, so you're easier to bully. You react with fear and frustration when dealing with nasty or difficult people. Sadly, everyone identifies your vulnerability to make an easy target or scape-goat and enjoy pushing your sensitive buttons.

Non-assertive people

Some people are trained to be submissive to obtain approval from others. Do you invest trust in your managers but are scared to discuss, confront or tackle difficult issues with them? Perhaps you claim you respect those in authority, but actually you fear them. If you don't know how to confront, tolerate or manipulate, you're forced to tolerate difficult people. You repress or bottle your anger, devalue your painful feelings, and explode later on. You relinquish your power and allow yourself to become easy prey for bullies and their cohorts. Sadly, sometimes you protect yourself by conforming to the ruling elite, betraying colleagues and supporting the bully against other targets.

Padlocked to the job

> *Cathy unsuccessfully applied for other jobs but was seen as being too close to retirement age. Her husband had retired due to poor health and their financial future was reliant on her working for a few more years. She was stuck and her bully knew it.*

There are many reasons why people can't leave their jobs. You may be passionate about your work and value the organisation's core purpose, such as helping others in need. You may be close to retirement, working in a specialised career, or have limited local job opportunities. It's difficult to leave a valued career, financial security and social group and jeopardise your professional and financial future. You may feel forced to stay because you've lost the confidence to apply elsewhere, or you're too injured to move or can't obtain a decent reference from your bully manager. The cunning bully knows they can bully you and get away with it.

Inertia

Some people only consult a doctor or a dentist when it's an emergency. The battered wife constantly forgives her abusive husband. Although you're aware of your discomfort and have tried to accommodate it, perhaps you hope the bully will leave, change or become respectful or that management will implement constructive, collaborative interventions. Unless there are solid reasons to play a waiting game (see *Bully Blocking at Work*; Field, 2010) until you can leave, you can find lots of naïve reasons for doing nothing; this includes being overwhelmed with fear, frustration, confusion and powerlessness. This means you become stuck, and so you wait until it escalates. Then you seek help, demand justice or take action when it's too late and you've been injured, temporarily or permanently.

Breaking point

> *The day that Dina discovered her bully had physically attacked his gay lover, she broke down and couldn't return to work.*

Some targets survive somehow for years — until they cannot cope any longer. This is when you break down or refuse to return to work; it may be due to one final aggressive confrontation or an accumulation of events. Alternatively, management wins and you are forced to undergo impulsive performance reviews, discriminatory disciplinary procedures, you experience further humiliation when they force you to undergo an unqualified psychiatric evaluation before you return to work or you are made redundant. You can regard these actions as a sign of systemic breakdown, poor management skills and symbolic of their lack of respect for employees.

Your therapist can help you identify and understand the gradual acceleration of the bullying and your breaking point. Don't blame yourself; you did your best under the circumstances, until enough was enough.

Why do people tolerate being bullied for so long?

There are many reasons people don't take action to confront their bullies or to leave. Here are some of the reasons that stopped my clients from taking action:

- It is really difficult to prove subtle bullying, especially when employers only value legal evidence, poorly trained investigators ignore their witnesses, and everyone denies their major physical, psychological and social symptoms.
- They believe they are the only target so no-one will take notice.
- They wait until it is too late.
- They lack assertive communication skills to confront the bully.
- They believe they are blameless and should not have to do anything.
- They expect someone else will intervene, such as a union, human resources or external investigator.
- They are scared to admit their emotional injuries.

- They fear, often correctly, that reporting will cause further intimidation, humiliation and retribution.
- The current work culture of fear or apathy fosters their 'learned helplessness' (Seligman, 1975).
- They hope their situation will improve.
- They love everything about their job, except the bullying and don't want to 'rock the boat.'
- They believe that if they leave, the others have won.

Identify your faulty beliefs and face facts

It seems that, many years ago, some poorly designed coping strategies were programmed into your brain. They were useful then, but are past their use-by-date now. You need to trash these old disks and replace them with more effective ones. Here are some of the out-of-date coping strategies you should trash:

The idea that loyal employees don't get hurt

You said to yourself: Things will work out; they wouldn't do that to me; justice will be done.

Fact: Despite your loyalty, your employer condones or can't manage bullying, betrays you when you request help and denies a fair resolution, meanwhile during this process, your symptoms are exacerbated.

'I think I can'

You may know the story of the little red train that climbed a steep hill. It kept on saying: *'I think I can, I think I can.'* Targets often say: *'I think I can, I think I can survive. I can cope, it's not that bad.'*

Fact: Although some women still walk miles for water, they would prefer a built-in tap. Maybe you can survive, but at what cost? Sometimes you only consider other options when forced to do so.

Excuses

You make enough excuses until you are paralysed into doing nothing. You blame yourself — *'I did something wrong.'* Forgive — *'They don't mean to hurt me.'* Rationalise — *'He's under pressure to reduce costs.'* Minimise — *'It's only a little thing.'* Justify — *'Everyone behaves like that.'* You praise — *'She can be nice and friendly at times and we used to get on so well.'*

Fact: Managers don't have to bully, nor does anyone else, it is unproductive. Others instinctively identify when they have zapped your power. Your excuses stop you identifying these inappropriate behaviours and blocking their harmful impact.

Friendship flipside

Mary was friendly with the manager until she made a suggestion regarding shifts. Her confrontation threatened him and he attacked.

Fact: Some friendships are built on submission. If you disagree or confront, the friendly connection breaks and conflict results. Your trusted workmate is unmasked as a manipulative or abusive game-player. Unfortunately, you trusted the wrong person or could not manage them effectively or their needs involved sabotaging yours.

Constant battle

Paul, a Catholic priest, once worked for a Monsignor who bullied everyone. Paul described it as a battle of wills every day. Sometimes he said nothing, other times he fought back. It was stressful and exhausting to manage, block and confront the Monsignor, even though he knew what to do. Eventually he gave up and moved interstate.

Fact: Cleaning up after a bunch of messy children every day or tidying up after another earthquake is tiring. Even if you can confront bullies assertively, dealing with bullying is exhausting and damaging.

Caring for others, not oneself

The rate of bullying appears higher in the welfare, medical and educational professions. Professional caregivers, ranging from nurses, teachers, and psychologists to surgeons work in careers where the client, patient or student receives expert caring, while they are being bullied by their companies, colleagues and consumers.

Fact: While conscientious, committed employees care for others, they can be bullied by incompetent managers and poorly advised irresponsible boards of management, if they disregard their own health and wellbeing.

Reframe your faulty myths

When we face facts and identify reality, we are able to take action. This is called reframing. Consider whether you could reframe any of the ideas on the left-hand column below with the words from the right-hand column.

'I must exceed my job requirements.'   *'I'll do what I'm paid to do.'*

'Everyone should achieve their best.'   *'I will work harder if I'm valued.'*

'Networking isn't necessary.'   *'I could socialise with key people.'*

'I have to be nice and passive.'   *'Assertive people are respected.'*

'My organisation should value me.'   *'I'm responsible for my health and wellbeing.'*

'I've always been a target.'   *'I can learn how to become assertive.'*

'Workmates should support me.'   *'They just value their professional security.'*

'We have bullying policies.'   *'My company seldom implements these policies.'*

'There should be teamwork.'   *'Old boys' clubs and women's cliques dominate.'*

'Bullying produces better results.'   *'It undermines staff and sabotages performance.'*

'Being sacked is shocking.'   *'I can explore all my options and move on.'*

REFLECTIVE MOMENT

Don't bully or blame yourself. Circle three to five reasons for why you've been bullied from the list below.

- Wrong time, wrong place
- Childhood experiences
- My personality — submissive or provocative
- Lack of assertion skills
- Bully's personality — for example, oblivious, attention-seeking, under pressure, sociopath
- *'My status is lower than the bully's'*
- *'I'm different to everyone else'*
- Personal difficulties, life experiences, limited social skills make me vulnerable
- It's cheaper to bully than to sack or make staff redundant
- *'My competence and conscientiousness threatens them'*
- *'I didn't build a strong support network and refused to suck up'*
- *'I misread the political situation and organisational problems at work'*
- *'My managers don't value all employees, only their mates'*
- Lack of effective management/leadership skills at work
- Legislation doesn't deter bullying
- *'My union was powerless'*
- Investigators/conciliators lack adequate training or power
- *'It is too expensive for me take legal action'*
- *'I can't "out" them on the Internet because they could sue'*
- The board of directors denies their legal responsibilities to create a safe workplace
- Medico–legal reports still misconstrue medical and psychological evidence, and thereby support bullies
- Society attacks the most vulnerable by blaming victims, not perpetrators.

Strategy 2 in brief

Understanding why you are being bullied is useful. It helps you take the correct action to end it. Your own faulty beliefs may inadvertently play a part in the problem. There are various reasons targets of bullying delay taking action for a long time. What are yours? To take action, find the reasons but don't blame yourself. Identify your breaking point.

CHAPTER FOUR

Strategy 3: Revalue and restore your identity

❝ *Some time ago I experienced a debilitating blood disorder. It forced me to go slow and travel inside my body. Exploring this relatively unknown territory was as strange as looking under my car bonnet! I've always focused on being an obliging provider, a good daughter, wife, mother, sister, friend, employee, colleague and psychologist. Slowly I became aware that, while pleasing and caring for others, I had neglected my internal needs. Although I valued my achievements, I forgot to care for my inner core. I realised that my body reflected my internal and external stressors. It broke down while I was researching stressful material about workplace bullying. Once I recovered, I bought an antique 'forget-me-not' ring and I wear it every day. It's a constant reminder to value myself.* **❞**

Bullying injures self-esteem

We live in an age where people judge one another by visible signs of success. Your appearance, phone, designer handbag, watch, car and lifestyle reflects your professional and financial achievements. While establishing your career, building your professional status and achieving material benefits, you may have neglected the need to value yourself, your health, family, friends and life. While investing more in your external identity, you invested less in your personal identity.

Being bullied (or even being a witness to bullying) can seriously injure your self-esteem. If your career and consequently other parts of your life have been severely affected, you may denigrate and devalue yourself. If you underestimate your injuries and overestimate others' capacity to rectify matters and restore justice, you further reduce your self-esteem and ability to cope.

Unfortunately, lowered self-esteem has a negative effect on your communication skills. You may find it difficult to tell your story in a plausible way, consequently people don't believe your version and become become less willing to help. However, you can improve your self-esteem, and then package and present your story with greater credibility. In this way you can create better opportunities for those with real power to assist you, such as managers, human resources, union officials, lawyers, and the media.

Check your inner core

Originally you may have valued yourself but this became impossible as a bully slowly humiliated you, while your employer, manager and colleagues betrayed you. Alternatively, after a history of abuse, often beginning in childhood, you were conditioned to believe that it was wrong to value yourself and confront those who don't respect you. This left you with a blindspot that left you unprotected from bullies. Perhaps you were oblivious to the true impact of the bullying or blamed yourself, rather than the bully, and became further injured. Even observing bullying is like breathing toxic air. Whatever your role in this macabre game, you can be affected.

Do you bully yourself?

Most school bullying targets are sensitive to certain issues. Their reactions to words like 'You're stupid' or 'You're gay' reveal their vulnerable points. They create and provide a bully with a well-worn path of self-criticism, making it easy for a lazy bully to follow. The bully picks up on their reactions to their own sensitive issues, nothing else.

Similarly, there is a strong possibility that your self-opinion is more self-critical than others. Perhaps your internal, judgmental bully forces you to absorb negative feedback from others without counteracting and counterbalancing their venom by validating your self-worth, or accepting compliments when they are deserved.

Therefore, you cannot allow bullying behaviours to become entwined with your own negative self-talk. This makes it really easy for bullies to strike, and perpetuates their bullying. Their attack route is clearly signposted. You are bullying yourself when you:

- expect to be perfect all the time and denigrate your mistakes
- regard mistakes as a failure, therefore totally unacceptable, rather than as a learning experience
- view feedback as an attack and become defensive
- habitually criticise or devalue yourself or others
- underestimate the severity of bullying
- assume that justice will prevail despite all the odds
- reject support and guidance from others
- punish yourself for not handling the bullying more effectively
- maintain a blind eye to your employer's lack of concern and incompetent management
- deny your other skills, resources and successes accumulated over a lifetime.

Identity and self-esteem

The development of self-esteem begins when a child feels loved and valued by their significant parenting figures: *I'm basically worthwhile because they love me*. After puberty you begin looking for your own identity and social acceptance. This will be influenced by your appearance, successes and difficulties, family support and social status at school. You will try to rebel against your parental figures and search for alternative heroes. Your self-esteem is positive when you can say: *I am me and I belong to a social tribe*.

If you had difficulties in your childhood, such as trauma, poor parenting or social problems, you may develop poor self-esteem. But if you attract caring mentors or manage to excel at sport, schoolwork or hobbies, you become resilient, survive and achieve. You move out of adolescence with a sense of: *I'm OK because I can do it.*

As you mature into adulthood your identity changes, incorporating many different roles. You can be a relative, employee, friend, football fan or cooking enthusiast. You say: *I have many roles.* But, if you just judge yourself by your career, not your whole being, then *Who I am* is replaced with: *My job makes me who I am.*

Many competent, successful people still feel insecure and undervalue themselves. Despite their achievements, their inner core has not changed much since childhood. This makes them a good target or bully. They say: *Despite my successes I feel worthless inside.* Alternatively, if you have never faced adversity, your survival skills are undeveloped and untested. You may say: *I'm OK as long as nothing goes wrong,* or *Bad things happen to other people, not to me.* This makes it hard for you to feel you are OK and resilient when something goes wrong.

You can't control your life

Perhaps at a deep level, being an adult is not as simple as you expected. You graduated from the innocence of childhood with a fantasy that you had total control over whatever happened to you and the power to deal with every problem. Workplace bullying forced you to reject naive beliefs about the world being a good and safe place and about your omnipotence. Confronting bullying means dealing with your own powerlessness, as well with organisational incompetence and injustice. No wonder you feel betrayed and lose self-esteem (Janoff-Bulman, 1992; Lutgen-Sandvik, 2008).

Accept who you are

Your self-core is the ability to accept who you are, with or without your make-up, e-mail provider, company car or fancy office. Your finger-print contains more than just your work profile. Like everyone else, you are a unique human being with flaws and failings. By the law of averages, everyone makes mistakes and confronts adversity, but there are just as many things that make you a good person. Although being bullied or losing a job is extremely threatening, your self-awareness and self-value should also depend upon many other parts of your life. Don't blame yourself, devalue your achievements or discredit yourself. Even though you are distressed, you need to focus on who you are, as distinct from your current job title as one day you may move on or retire. You cannot base your identity on any job alone or allow anyone to steal your whole identity.

Every cell in your body replaces itself regularly, including your hair, nails, skin and bone. Your body is genetically engineered to survive and adapt to change. You have the resources to deal with life's challenges. Accept yourself as you are, but figure out what changes you need to make to survive.

People with healthy self-esteem understand and accept who they are. They empower themselves by being flexible and finding new strategies to adapt to change. Their resilience is based upon their ability to confront the ups and downs of life. Even when they are not pleased with aspects of their personality or performance, they still value themselves. They absorb all feedback and seek alternative ways of surviving among hostile people. Everything is viewed as a constructive challenge. They try to change what they can, without becoming defensive or threatened.

Value yourself

When your self-esteem is healthy, you appreciate yourself. You value your needs, desires, beliefs and human rights. You know you are worthy of respect, safety and happiness. It means loving yourself as you are, with all your positive and negative attributes. Like a devoted parent or dog owner, this requires unconditional acceptance, understanding and forgiveness. Once you commit yourself to being self-caring and self-responsible, you can aim for what you want and enjoy your achievements. It's an internal process: *'I love me, despite everything happening in my life, and I'll care for myself and value my life.'*

When your self-esteem is healthy, you interpret the other person's behaviour as their problem and take responsibility for your own behaviours. You may also need to accept that your employer does not value good management skills, employee safety or productivity and therefore can't protect you.

Fantasy blockers

- Visualise an imaginary glass wall between yourself and the bully. Design its width and height, then imagine that, whatever they do, they cannot hurt you.
- Pretend that you are completely surrounded and protected by a wall of strong laser beams. If they come near they will get zapped or repelled by the laser.
- Picture the bully as a large human-shaped balloon (full of selfish ego). Prick the balloon and imagine seeing their bubble burst.
- Imagine the bully abuses an employee whose brother plays golf with the CEO. He moves the bully sideways, without company perks, and his career goes downhill.

Repair the injuries

> *After three years of hospital admissions, severe depression and self-harm, Jenny said, 'Bits of my old self are coming back'.*
>
> *Brendan took his team away for a few days to have fun and rebuild relationships after the bullying ended.*
>
> *Maggie found that cooking new recipes provided her with a sense of achievement.*
>
> *Bill found that planning a different career gave him a new identity.*

You need to repair the damage caused to your self-esteem by bullying, whether it feels like a small dent, a serious fracture or a complete implosion. Your self-esteem bank may be low, especially if you did not invest regularly, because then there is not much to withdraw. By finding ways to respect yourself, you will cope better with your workplace. You will be better equipped to assess your options, take action and move on.

Add value to your self-esteem

There are many ways to rebuild your self-esteem. Here are three simple ways.

1. Pamper and care for yourself

When you care for yourself, you neutralise toxic emotions and become more resilient. This means finding regular activities to value yourself and counteract self-criticism. Just as frequent-flyer schemes build up holiday points, remember that doing lots of little things is better than doing something rewarding every three months. Try to validate your self-esteem ticket three times day and make sure you use nature, family and friends as essential ingredients.

- Collect a pamper list — music, chocolate, massage, retail therapy.
- Take time out from stress — movies, reading, socialising with friends or family.
- Bring some fun and bling into your life — jewellery, unusual clothing, a new watch.

SMELL THE ROSES, LISTEN TO THE BIRDS, TASTE THE CHOCOLATE, HUG YOURSELF!

- Find feel-good activities — gardening, movies, nature walks, massage.
- Discover different enjoyable interests, games or hobbies.
- Give yourself validating labels — 'feisty', 'hero', 'warrior', 'survivor'.

2. Let others give to you

People who value themselves allow others to give them empathy, advice and support. Don't keep secrets from family and friends, and give them a regular but very brief update. Make sure you hear and value all the positive feedback you get.

- Value gifts from the universe: fresh roses along your footpath, friendly smiles, a sunny day, a caring phone call.
- Accept the support, constructive suggestions and useful connections that others offer: empathy, written witness statements, testimonials, another job.
- When family or friends offer financial support, accept when necessary.
- Ask others for feedback; record the positive, eliminate the negative and use constructive feedback to change your ineffective behaviours and move on.

3. Care for others

People who have good support networks tend to cope better and live longer. When you give friendship, care and empathy to others, the universe returns it to you. As you reciprocate, you will feel respected, valued or loved in return. When you are friendly to all work colleagues, you are less likely to be excluded, isolated and devalued.

- Remember that friends, family and neighbours enjoy chitchat and socialising with you.
- When family and friends have problems, they need empathy. Although you lack energy to be completely caring, verbalise your concern for them, such as *I'm sad to hear that you are going through this*. Hopefully it will take your mind off your problems and you will feel better.

- Show interest in your workmates and acquaintances. They have a life outside work as well. Chat about their issues and interests, or neutral subjects such as sport, shopping, and travel.

- Do some voluntary work; you will feel better helping those less fortunate. You may get a reference, perhaps even a job. Alternatively, help out friends. For example, Barb is handy with a hammer and does odd jobs for friends; Dina and Katie helped Leah write to the media about bullying; Bev helped Carla move house after the bullying.

Self-esteem boosters

There are lots of other ways you can build your self-esteem and value yourself. They can include:

Anchors

Anchors bring back good memories of special events and provide positive feelings. They refresh, reinforce and rebuild confidence. You may feel better wearing certain clothing — for example, velvet, jewellery, or a certain brand name. Some people use gemstones, others are anchored to their iPhones or Blackberries. Trish kept singing the song by Tina Turner, *You're simply the best, better than all the rest*, which helped her though a hard time.

Empower your appearance

The Italian concept of *la bella figura*, or making a good impression, underpins nearly every aspect of Italian society. Italians believe that despite any difficulties in their private lives, they must present an image of success to the world.

Most workplaces expect you to wear a certain style of clothing. Whether you wear jeans or a suit, changing into work clothes automatically propels you into work mode. Like a uniform, your clothing transmits messages about who you are and how you wish to be treated. Your clothes reveal whether you belong to the tribe or you are an outsider. You may inadvertently threaten others with your elegant appearance, or undervalue yourself by dressing too plainly.

People who begin to appear frequently on television change their style of dressing to suit the public screen. Likewise, you can adapt your style of dressing to protect and empower yourself. You can appear younger and trendy, or older and dated. A good makeover will make you appear more assertive. Although you cannot completely hide your age, stress and work difficulties, your appearance will influence work colleagues.

By changing your clothes or accessories, you can create a stronger look. Trendy clothes and suits are empowering; gimmicky, glitzy clothing gets noticed and dowdy clothing is a camouflage. You can choose when you want to be hidden or be seen.

You can use colours to alter your mood. Although fashion and culture influence colours, some people feel cheerful in yellow, peaceful in mauve, relaxed in green, energised in red and neutral in black. It does not matter what you wear, as long as it works and does not threaten anyone.

Your confidence makeover may include:

- fashionable clothes, up-to-date hairstyle, hair colour, makeup: '*I'm like you. I'm visible and credible.*'
- using a strong perfume or after-shave: '*I smell differently, stay away.*'
- wearing brightly coloured or sexy underwear: '*I feel cheeky inside.*'
- trying unusual mobile phone tones, funky watches: '*I'm fun, not threatening.*'
- using flamboyant ties, shirts, jewellery, bright lipstick/nail polish, odd socks/shoelaces to get noticed: '*I'm exciting to be around.*'
- wearing flowing clothes, long scarves, dangling jewellery, bright lipstick and nails: '*I like attention and social networking.*'

Understand confidence

Perhaps you think that you need some more confidence to rebuild your self-esteem and say: '*I will feel good about myself when I get my confidence back.*' However, searching for confidence is like looking for the end of a rainbow and more elusive than looking for happiness. Maybe the idea of altering your confidence levels seems odd. You might say: '*This isn't me.*' Well, who is it? I doubt if you are the same person at work as you are on holidays. You would be very different if you won millions of dollars in a lottery. You constantly change your thoughts and behaviours to adapt to what is happening around you.

Once you look confident, people respect you more. Despite your stresses you can pretend and fake it till you make it (Cuddy, Cuddy, & Yap, 2010), or behave as if you have confidence. Like learning anything new, it may feel uncomfortable at first. As you practise, you will slowly master the way to do it naturally. You will find that whether you actually feel safe or just pretend, you will instantly look and feel better.

Build mastery

When you are overwhelmed with a bullying game, without employer support, you can forget how capable you really are. All through your life you have mastered many different challenges. Some were simple, such as tying shoelaces; others were complicated, like combining work, study

---

REFLECTIVE MOMENT

Sit down somewhere quiet and visualise some of the activities you have mastered:

- As a child — making your lunch, riding a bike, doing chores and homework.

- As an adolescent — using public transport, dealing with peers, exploring your sexuality.

- As an adult — coping with a new job, doing home renovations, maintaining a special relationship, planning an extensive holiday, coping with difficult family members.

and a family. You have mastered many skills but you have forgotten this because you do them so successfully that they have become automatic.

Although you are feeling handicapped at work, try to develop skills in other areas to boost your confidence. From growing herbs to trying new recipes, these skills can offer you a revitalised sense of achievement, renewed energy and improved self-esteem.

Empowering words

Some words can have a long-lasting impact upon us. Stand in front of a mirror. Look, act and sound confident. Tell the person in the mirror that you accept yourself unconditionally: *'I'm great. I'm OK. I am worthy just as I am.'*

- Make a mantra: *'I will take action. I won't let anyone abuse me. If I don't accept defeat, I can't be defeated. I can survive this. This too will pass.'*

- Find a metaphor: *'Jenny weaves a spider's web.' 'Julie thinks she is a good manager, she kicks arse.' 'Jack uses his dick not his head.' 'Jill says that work was like a maze. She went in and got lost.'*

- Use a proverb: *'Don't let the bastards get you.' 'Always know who and where your enemies are.' 'A seed has to crack before it can grow.' 'When money speaks, the truth keeps silent.' 'He's an open book but some of the pages are stuck together.' 'I'm a rooster, not a feather duster.' 'A trouble shared is a trouble halved.' 'Today's crocodile is tomorrow's handbag.' 'My workplace is a cross between a cult and the mafia.' 'Those whom you hurt on the way up may retaliate on your way down.' 'You can't make an omelette without breaking eggs.' 'Olives are crushed to make olive oil, diamonds are cut to reveal their brilliance.'*

Rituals

Rituals are regular daily or weekly activities. Some are personal or family-based, some symbolise significant events while some represent your religious or cultural background. They signify affiliation, provide boundaries and reduce anxiety. Perhaps you can identify those you have already and create some more. Don't blame yourself; you did your best under the circumstances, until enough was enough.

- Smile and chitchat to everyone at work, in and around your workplace.
- Offer to make tea/coffee for fellow workers.
- Time out — go for a walk every lunchtime; find some quiet time at night.
- Record — write down significant issues from the day.
- Regular daily meditation, mantra or prayer.
- Develop a better sleep ritual — bathroom, brush teeth, wash face, light reading, a drink, valerian or lavender on pillow and lights off.

Reality check

Write down the positive and negative aspects of your life. Compare the list. For example:

Positive	Negative
I have good employment skills.	*It's hard to find a secure job.*

Find a different focus

> *Michael was a dedicated public servant. When his supervisor retired, he applied for his job. The new manager gave it to a mate from her former workplace. Michael was angry and hurt; his self-esteem was 'shot to pieces'. He felt he had been shafted by a person with less experience. He told me the approach he was taking to survive the disappointment: 'I decided not to put all my eggs in one basket. There's more to life than your employer. I need to keep a balanced outlook and focus on other things so that work issues don't dominate my life.' He began playing squash twice a week and found other interests. He's doing the minimum at work, waiting for a good redundancy package or retirement.*

While a ballerina pirouettes many times on her toes, she keeps her eye focused on a definite point, otherwise she would become dizzy and fall over. You also need to maintain your internal balance and keep focused. In the best scenario, the bullying is acknowledged and the workplace is made safe. Some employees obtain justice and compensation or quit and find another job. However, not everyone can leave when they want to, so you need to find other ways to cope with the bullying. You can study something different, take up a new hobby or find a new career. When you shift your focus you may decide to make real changes in your life.

REFLECTIVE MOMENT

Find some time and a comfortable place to consider the meaning of your job and its significance in your life. Remember there is more to your week than just work.

• What were your dreams at 12 years of age?

• What were your goals during the past 10 years?

• What are your achievements in this job?

• What personal and career goals do you want to achieve by the time you are 70?

• Compare this job to your five most important goals, such as family, friends, financial, recreation, community service.

• What else do you want to achieve in your life, and what do you enjoy doing?

• What small steps can you take towards achieve your goals?

• What can you do to begin your journey into a new direction?

Strategy 3 in brief

Bullying at work injures your self-esteem as a target, witness or bully. Try to discover the reasons why your self-esteem has become injured, such as earlier experiences, unrealistic expectations, values and beliefs. Then find simple ways to reprogram your self-negativity, accept yourself as you are, or change what you can and reinforce your positive self-esteem by giving to yourself, incorporating feedback and giving care to others.

CHAPTER FIVE

Strategy 4:
Use effective
communication skills

“Kim was shy and badly bullied at school. He stayed because of his friends, although they didn't support him or confront the bullies. After leaving school he thought he'd left the bullying behind. To his horror, he was bullied at college and at work. He thought the word 'victim' was written in large letters across his forehead. When his parents brought him for counselling he was unmotivated and oblivious to his poor communication skills. After a few sessions I decided to use my video camera. After seeing himself on the video, he realised that he exacerbates any situation by looking and behaving like a target. Three sessions later, he'd changed. He smiled more often, spoke clearly and appeared more confident. Since then he has learnt to deal more effectively with difficult people, without retreating or becoming angry. The added bonus is that by protecting himself and using effective communication skills, he is respected by others, more confident and having a better social life.”

Every group or culture develops its own codes of behaviour to maintain their tribal connections. They reflect the tribe's traditional way of communicating, revealing each person's intention to belong to that tribe or not. The way you communicate and relate to one another is reflected in these rules. For example, people in western cultures use eye contact and smile to show friendliness. They are encouraged to express their feelings. In contrast, most people born in Asian countries tend to use less eye contact and show a plain face instead of revealing their feelings.

People who use the tribe's basic communications skills effectively, are regarded as sociable and friendly. They say what they mean and their body language reflects what they are saying. It is easy to tell when they are being friendly, respectful and non-threatening, or whether they don't care, may attack or have switched off.

Communication skills are vital for working and socialising. They demonstrate your ability to connect authentically with others as well as your vulnerabilities and strengths. But even when you have good communication skills, they may fail you when you are being bullied. You may look frustrated, defensive or vulnerable, for example, or take on poor posture, gritted teeth or clenched fists. Subtle behaviours like blushing, poor eye contact and quivering lips may betray your difficulty in managing the situation.

Faulty communication skills handicap you in relating to anyone, especially difficult, challenging work colleagues. The average bully intuitively realises when you are vulnerable and this encourages them to continue their game. If you are passive or aggressive, you cannot convey your message assertively. If you express yourself poorly, you instil doubt and insecurity in those who work for or with you. This can exacerbate your situation and threaten your work tribe, who can lose respect for you.

Recent research by the Massachusetts Institute of Technology (Dingfelder, 2010) shows that social interaction involves more regions of the brain than previously thought, and the right superior temporal sulcus — an area that interprets other's actions — is especially active. Hopefully, future research will show how different sections of the brain process social information and assist us to develop appropriate treatment strategies.

Regardless of whether your work culture is controlled by respect or fear, effective communication skills help you cope with challenging people without upsetting the status quo. There is no benefit in pretending to be confident or taking action without using assertive communication skills, including courageous chats, constructive conversations or confronting questions that guarantee some accountability, demonstrating whether you are valued or not.

Even if you are feeling vulnerable inside, these skills convey a constructive message. They reduce your likelihood of being targeted, allow you to confront others respectfully, block any bullying, undermine abusive employees, inform the relevant authorities with conviction, and develop collaborative, protective networks.

I believe that developing effective communication skills is an important part of managing workplace bullying. You can establish the type of respect you gave some of your primary school teachers who walked into your classroom with absolute confidence, and your supplementary bonus is that bullies are more likely to avoid people who are friendly, socially gregarious and relate well to those at work who don't condone any bullying.

The communication game

You need to match your communication strategies to your particular work group. If tribal members are caring and collaborative, be sincere, genuine and authentic. When it is safe to confront, use the assertive 'I' language to express your thoughts and feelings. Don't blame or be scared of saying the wrong thing and upsetting someone. When you are honest and give instant feedback to insensitive people, they generally respect you more; in fact, popular people express themselves clearly.

However, if colleagues are being adversarial, protect yourself without being rude or aggressive. You need a false facade with serial bullies to disguise your emotions and appear cool, neutral and pleasant (remember, it makes them happy when you reveal fear or anger), whereas you can behave in a friendly, feisty and forthright manner with some non-malicious bullies. Overall, you need to remain pleasant, sociable and firm when dealing with employees who use bullying behaviours.

Learning new skills

I have a book for dog owners called, *Walkies in Victoria.* Dogs cannot read, but their owners can, so the author writes in the language we use with our dogs. Likewise, you have probably heard people use a childish voice with toddlers, or speak slowly to migrants and speak loudly while using their mobile phone. Everyone uses different styles of communicating to adapt to a situation, depending on where they are and to whom they are speaking; thus a chat over coffee is different to a media interview or business presentation.

I want you to improve your communication skills. Don't refuse and say, *But that's who I am and what I do.* You, too, use different styles in different places, and you may need to update your appropriate communication style for your workplace. The bonus is that improved communication skills can empower you in all other areas of your life.

Communication skills

Successful communication is visual, vocal and verbal. The skills can be subtle or obvious. Albert Mehrabian's (1981) research shows that 55% of communication is body language, 38% is voice and 7% is words. Thus the bulk of communication is nonverbal. Regardless of the actual percentage, clearly what you actually convey non-verbally is more meaningful than your words. Be alert to inconsistencies in their words, voice or body language, this feedback is a warning sign.

My recipe for effective communication skills, provided it is culturally sensitive, will empower you at work, home or elsewhere. It is a behavioural technology, based upon neuro-linguistic programming.

When you are being challenged do you show:

Confident behaviour	Unconfident behaviour
Make clear eye contact	Look everywhere else
Show a pleasant, neutral look	Appear stunned, distressed, angry, scared
Stand straight	Jiggle like a teabag
Speak clearly and calmly	Speak quietly or mumble

Use humour or assertive words	Attack or become defensive
Incorporate non-verbal feedback	Disregard or misread feedback
Express your feelings directly	Bottle feelings inside
Confront immediately	Delay or withhold appropriate feedback.

Communication skills toolkit

Breathing skills

When you are relaxed, you breathe deeply and slowly. When you are scared or angry, you breathe in short breaths. Bullies, like animals, will sense any irregular pattern of breathing. When they think that you are anxious, they will react accordingly and attack. The trick is to focus on breathing in a relaxed manner to appear more assertive. Practise this regularly.

Show confidence

Most people are terrified of speaking publicly but, like children in front of doting grandparents, rise to the occasion when necessary. For example, they may look very confident if the media interviews them about witnessing an accident. Everyone knows instinctively how to behave — stand up straight, speak clearly and look the interviewer in the eye. Imagine that you are going public about bullying in work-places. How would you stand, sound and behave? You can do it!

Practise the skills

Although professional speakers sound natural and spontaneous, they practise their stories regularly in front of a mirror, the wall or with their dogs. Nobody learns a new skill immediately; it takes time and practice to become automatic. Although assertive language may feel foreign, it needs to be rehearsed until you know how to stand, use eye contact, a firm, pleasant voice, and the appropriate words. The next time you are confronted by a difficult person, allow a confident voice to pop out. Your new approach can block their power — just look at how others actually do it.

Get mentoring

Ask your family, friends, work colleagues or therapist for constructive feedback about your communication skills. You may need a mentor or voice coach. A video camera is excellent for learning skills. You could attend courses on dealing with difficult people, assertiveness skills or social skills.

Use humour

A friend, Jean-Pierre, has an extremely 'camp' way of saying '*Hello, hello!*' when he makes a comment or asks a rhetorical question. He uses a deeper voice, moves a shoulder forward, raises his eyebrows and blinks his eyes rapidly. Nobody is offended and they laugh. Whereas my Italian friend Antoinetta has a wonderful of saying '*Whatever, whatever*'. She simultaneously shakes her hands and shoulders, moves her head from side to side in a subtle manner and dismisses the subject.

Eye skills

When you make eye contact with another person eyeball to eyeball, you stand up straighter, breathe in more oxygen and appear less anxious. You make more room for your voice to resonate in your chest, so you look and sound more confident. You don't need to stare; just show people that you are really interested in them. When you maintain good eye contact it empowers you, enables intimacy and reinforces your self-esteem. Simultaneously, you can assess their feedback and determine whether it is friendly, feisty, foolish or foul. This is part of your survival kit.

Eye ideas

- Focus your eyes like darts to 'laser' someone abusive.
- Develop a variety of stares, such as curious, blank, aggressive, amazement.
- Don't stare at the ground, the wall or jiggle your eyes like searchlights.
- Widen your eyes, alter your blinking rate to confuse them, try eyebrow push-ups.

Face skills

Facial expressions are basically the same all over the world, for all tribes and cultures. Imagine that your face is like the instrument panel of an aeroplane; it can reveal nearly everything you think or feel. It has many fine facial muscles to communicate your message. For example, you use 17 muscles to smile and 43 muscles to frown. Practise some different facial expressions.

Neutral face

Sometimes it is unwise to show your feelings to a serial bully, even if you are assertive. The neutral face contains no emotion, like a poker player, which makes it very hard for aggressive or defensive people to react or retaliate. You can present a polite, blank mask by training your facial muscles.

- Look cool and calm but ready to spring into action when necessary.
- Adopt a trance-like, bored or spaced-out look.
- Look casual, relaxed and floppy, like a dog on a hot summer's day.
- Imagine that you are a geisha, sentry guard or stand-up comedian.

Active face

You appear genuine and assertive when you display your thoughts and feelings on your face in an authentic, animated manner. It is a prerequisite for establishing friendship and maintaining intimacy with friends, family or trusted workmates, provided you also connect and show care.

- Manage your fine facial muscles to reflect your feelings, such as concern, confusion, and frustration.
- Match your facial gestures to your body language, voice and words.
- Relax your facial muscles, especially your eyes, jaws and cheeks, allowing them to move naturally as regulated by your feelings.
- Move your lips to emphasise a point and communicate your message.
- When you are feeling tense your lips will droop, mumble or appear tense because you are pressing them together. So when you are in a

difficult situation do the opposite — relax your lips and part them slightly. Your energy level will move from tense to calm and you will appear more self-confident.

- Don't hide behind your glasses; make sure your facial expressions are seen, or else unfathomable.
- Don't worry about blushing (use make-up, blame the heat or a spicy meal).

Smiles

Smiling helps you to think and feel better because it brings more blood to the brain. Smiles vary from looking warm, pleased and genuine to a nice, bland, square sort of smile. You can practise them in front of a mirror.

- The active smile conveys friendship, respect and demonstrates confidence.
- The nice (square) smile looks stuck and superficial but blocks any connection.
- The passive smile looks 'nice' and safe but you actually appear vulnerable and weak, scared and powerless.

Body skills

> When Gina was in a business meeting she felt empowered when she behaved like a male: she placed her arms behind her head, took up the whole space of the chair, spreading her arms and legs wide, her head up. She would close her eyes a little bit or look out of the window as though she was bored.

When you interact with others, your body reflects what you think and feel inside. It's not about the content of the message, but how you're communicating it. If you are feeling powerless your behaviours show agitation or paralysis. If your body language resembles limp celery, a jiggling teabag or rigid soldier then it shows vulnerability. This is like waving a red rag to a bully or vulnerable target. Their survival instinct cannot predict if you will fight or flee, so they attack first.

Cuddy et al. (2010) found that: 'Adopting powerful postures allows people to prepare for stressful situations and confidently take risks due to their psychological, physiological and behavioural changes' (p. 1363) thus people have the ability to 'fake it 'til they make it'. These minimal postural changes and their outcomes can potentially improve a person's general health, wellbeing and confidence. The only way you can look confident and assertive is by standing, moving or sitting in a relaxed, controlled but supple manner, like a dancer or athlete.

- Don't jiggle your body, fiddle with objects, or adjust hair or clothing.
- Limp handshakes reflect insecurity — firm handshakes convey power.
- If they are using threatening movements, don't cower, just stand upright and stare.
- If they are towering over you, then tell them to sit down, stand up yourself, or tell them that you need eye contact and stand on a stool.

Body space

Australia is a big country with small pockets of population, so Aussies are accustomed to wide-open spaces. This is reflected in the space between them when they meet. In many other countries there is less open space and larger populations, so most people stand or sit closer together.

- Manipulate the space between you and others to adjust the comfort level up or down.

- Imagine going close to someone difficult and saying, *'I'm a little deaf can you say that louder?'* (so that bystanders can witness their behaviours).

- Instead of bending forwards towards them, try a very subtle bend backwards. You might appear more confident.

Voice

Your voice is a powerful communication tool that establishes your identity and credibility. Just as your accent and dialect display your origins, a strained, fragile, frustrated voice demonstrates fear, annoyance, powerlessness and confusion. Mumbling makes you sound weak and passive, a babyish or nasal voice lowers your credibility, while a high-pitched voice makes you sound nervous and timid — far less powerful than those with deeper voices.

Even small birds can sing very loudly. It is useless to say something clever that nobody can hear. You need to speak clearly and succinctly so that everyone understands what you have to say. When you use an animated, strong voice, you appear assertive and authoritative and need these communication techniques to manage bullies.

Voice tricks

> Bill is the manager of a large trucking company. He was sick and tired of being bullied by the union fellow, so when he screamed, Bill spoke quietly.

- When you animate your voice and express emotion, you sound genuine.

- Make your voice sound strong and grounded.

- Use downward inflections to sound knowledgeable and less insecure.

- Speak with a neutral, monotone voice to hide any emotion

- No-one forgets the voice of a strong primary teacher in response to childish tantrums, so use a similar voice and say: *'This isn't an appropriate time to discuss this matter, I'll come back later.'*

- Check that you are not speaking too fast or too slow.
- If they yell, match their tone by projecting your voice and then lower it slowly, without becoming aggressive.
- Emphasise certain words to make your point — for example: '*I will take **action** if this **happens** again*', '*I don't like being **yelled** at*', or '*I'm unhappy about **your** toxic vibes infecting this **workplace**'.

Silence

> You will learn that silence is a powerful strategic weapon. It can be very effective. The last bully I dealt with almost ran away from me because I held her accountable by using silence. Another advantage is that your words can't come back to haunt you.

Nobody likes silence, so you can control people by creating a space or vacuum between yourself and them. Imagine saying: '*I'm listening*' then pause or wait; thereby pressuring them to respond.

Words

Assertive talk

Although you may believe that your thoughts and feelings are transparent, in fact, it can be difficult for colleagues to recognise exactly what you are thinking and feeling. Thus it may be hard for them to understand exactly what is happening to you and then respond appropriately. Your words may need to become more accurate, specific and honest to reflect exactly what your feelings are.

When you begin a sentence with 'I' you express whatever you think, feel and want. It provides truth and authenticity to your words, makes you assume responsibility for whatever you communicate and empowers you. It is an easy form of communicating and does not blame, attack, threaten or force others to become defensive. This emotional honesty gives you options in dealing with people. But don't be fooled by its simplicity. Few people do it effectively and consistently, at work or anywhere else.

Be aware there are differences in dealing with school and workplace bullying. You may feel safe to tell another adult: '*Please stop, I don't like this bullying behaviour.'* They may will respond with embarrassment, an apology, defensiveness or attack. But never allow your kids to say it. This makes school bullies happy. Children need retorts for bullies unless they are confronting their real friends.

Aggressive language — 'You'

When you use this form of expression you blame, threaten and sound aggressive — *'You shouldn't speak to me like that.'*

Passive language — 'They'

This type of expression makes you appear vague, confused and power-less — *'Managers know they shouldn't do that.'*

Assertive language — 'I'

You empower yourself with assertive language — *'I'm feeling frustrated by your constant swearing.' 'It is not appropriate for me to do that right now.'*

The big bonus

Assertive talk has another fantastic outcome. The moment you use the 'I' word, you receive instant verbal and nonverbal feedback. You find out exactly what the listener feels about you, because this process makes them accountable. Their feedback reveals whether they care or don't care about your feelings. Then you can plan your next step, including all the options mentioned in *Bully Blocking at Work* (Field, 2010). Beware that, just like the caring parent who cannot satisfy all their children's wishes, the other person may be caring, but may not be able to satisfy all your work requirements.

The 'I' statement

'I think that ... ' — decide what you would like to share with people at work, including a bully, the target of the bully, your manager, human resources, and senior management. Their response to you demonstrates what they think about your statement.

- *'I think some people are undermining this team. Can anyone tell me why and what can be done?'*

- *'My last performance review was excellent — I think you're targeting me by sabotaging this recent performance review.'*
- *'I don't understand why the shifts are not allocated fairly.'*
- *'I meant no offence, are you upset with me?'*
- *'I'm not arrogant, but I do enjoy the statistical probability of receiving praise a few times a year.'*
- *'I saw you roll your eyes at me, can you tell me why?'*

'I feel …' — once you understand what your feelings about the situation, share them with significant others at work or home. Some people don't consciously mean to hurt, so if you don't express what you feel, the bullying can continue. The immediate response reveals whether they care, apologise and stop, or whether they don't care and will not stop.

- *'I feel annoyed that staff are undermining productivity here with their malicious gossip.'*
- *'I'm angry that you always micro-manage me and allow other staff to exclude me from important events.'*
- *'I'm scared that you are blaming her without any evidence and without speaking to every witness.'*
- *'I feel upset that you always criticise me while praising others.'*

'I would like …' — in many workplaces people have the right to express what they want or need. Then you can discuss, negotiate or confront, as long as you remain respectful. While there is no guarantee of success, it is an opportunity for feedback. Responses from others clearly demonstrate whether they respect and care for you or don't care and will sabotage you.

- *'I would like constructive criticism; screaming doesn't help me improve my performance.'*
- *'I would like you to include everyone in this team, not just the popular group.'*
- *'I understand there have been complaints. I would like to see them in writing so I can take the appropriate action.'*

Action talk

> In our family, Ruben was the extrovert. The moment he entered a room he would stand still, smile and greet everyone, whereas Evelyn, an introvert, sidles in and sits down. Eventually, she lifts her eyes to smile and connect with others individually, moves around to greet those she knows and then chats to strangers.

The value of action talk is that it demonstrates to others that you want to connect, relate and work together to solve challenging work issues, rather than threatening or challenging them, which sabotages everyone. It is the essential workplace lubricant, establishing a bond of communication and conciliation to collaborate and resolve workplace difficulties, in order that everyone can benefit from being employed in a successful, productive workplace.

Ask questions

Questions show interest, care, concern and clarify issues. You can work out some appropriate work, social and personal questions to ask colleagues. As most people love to talk about themselves (their favourite subject), ask about their family, hobbies and recreation. I advise clients to have a collection of five generic, not-too-personal questions for each gender, such as sport or the economy for men, and shopping or favourite programs for women. While they are speaking, respond by doing some 'noddies', like a television interviewer does.

Chitchat

> According to a Hollywood film producer, four major film studios were chaired by women at one stage. Instead of board meetings beginning with a traditional chat about sport, they now begin with subjects like, 'Where did you get your hair done?' or 'Where did you get those shoes?'

People use chitchat as a preliminary investigation to check each other out, discover mutual interests, maintain contact, connect and establish working alliances with supportive colleagues and the 'in-group' while avoiding enemies or the unpopular group. Eventually, chitchat may lead to closer, possibly more intimate friendships.

Making contact is easy for socially outgoing, friendly people, but it is extremely difficult for shy, introverted or traumatised people. In fact, some people regard chitchat as superficial, but it is actually a social necessity. It releases tension and informally allows others to hear what you are experiencing or witnessing at work, provided it is not malicious gossip. Bullies prefer to operate in secrecy; employees who chitchat to a larger audience may block their behaviours. Besides, friendly, chatty people are more likely to be regarded as 'normal' and thus accepted by their tribe, and may be more likely to obtain support along the company grapevine.

Show interest and empathy

When you show genuine interest in others and participate appropriately in their conversations, then you build connections. When you share your feelings and acknowledge those of others, you express empathy. This helps you build rapport and develop stronger, interpersonal connections. Later on, this may grow into emotional intimacy, which is important in times of crisis. Building relationships with other employees and managers improves teamwork and facilitates conflict resolution. In fact, Kraus, Cote and Keltner (2010, p. 1716) believe that 'being empathic provides a better ability to respond to social threats and gives you an opportunity to respond to social opportunities'. Generally, the more information you share with others without using or abusing them, the more they can help you. However, beware of those who will use anything against you once they are feeling threatened.

Conflict resolution skills

> Instead of reacting and becoming defensive, Pat looked Jack in the eye, listened quietly and stood upright. She lowered her voice, agreed with one point and explained her reasons for disagreeing with his nasty appraisal. She waited, but he had stopped.

Among any group of people, there are differences of opinion. The ideal scenario is where everyone involved collaborates to create a fair resolution. This is healthy and constructive if everyone has equal power and effective negotiation and conflict resolution skills. Unfortunately, if you have been squashed, taught to be nice, cannot handle threats, worry about the mob, work for an organisation that regards any challenge as a betrayal or prefers the adversarial approach, this is extremely difficult.

Most people avoid confrontation; they either internalise their distress or explode. Before working out whether to confront or not, assess the risks, such as infuriating a serial bully, exacerbating a volatile situation or losing more employees because of him.

Constructive questions:

- *'If I behaved differently, would everyone be nicer to me?'*
- *'What have I done to upset the staff around here?'*
- *'What can I change so that you can work with me in a more respectful manner?'*
- *'How do I rub people up the wrong way?'*

Confronting questions:

- *'I wonder who is manipulating or pressuring you- because of the way you treat others and myself?'*
- *'Do you understand the impact on me when you bully/exclude/micromanage/tease/humiliate me?'*
- *'Being truthful is fine, but show respect and empathy.'*
- *'I am sure you like honesty and saying what you think, but I find it easier when I understand how you feel.'*
- *'I know that you are sensitive but when you bark do you realise that others feel attacked?'*
- *'I don't like you doing ...'*
- *'I believe that you do not have any understanding about how your behaviours are affecting me.'*

Plan to work together

Have you ever met an acquaintance, shared some chitchat and said, 'Let's get together again?' If you are really keen, you call and make an arrangement, although most people wait for the other to ring first, so nothing happens. Then there are those who complain about never being invited over for a meal and wait without ever inviting others themselves!

Some people believe they work best alone, others think that men should stick together, that older workers are ignorant and useless and that conscientious, competent workers never make mistakes. The fact is, most companies improve and their employees achieve better results by using constructive feedback and collaborating as a team. Thus, you may need to establish closer links with colleagues and build teamwork. The good thing is that they will be more likely to support you when you need them.

The key word is 'let's'. For example

- *'Let's do this together.'*
- *'Can I get some help with this?'*
- *'Let's talk about work over coffee.'*
- *'I need help to deal with a bullying problem.'*
- *'What is your role in this project and what is mine?'*
- *'Let's make it fairer and trade tasks/shifts/work stations.'*

The key is feedback

You communicate successfully when you connect and cooperate with your listener. Your actual communication is the message they receive, not your intended one, which means separating the content from the process of communication. Your challenge is to convey a message that they receive — just as you intended. The only way you can find out is by observing their feedback and checking back whether they understood what you meant or not. Then you can modify your conversation strategies according to their feedback (John, 2009, personal communication).

Thus feedback from others acts like a mirror. It reflects your effective and ineffective behaviours, thus demonstrating how you can improve your communication skills. If feedback is false, just trash it. If a manager fabricates performance or disciplinary issues to avoid dealing with a bullying complaint or does not realise that your performance level has deteriorated because of the bullying, find evidence to support you.

If it is true but uncomfortable, assess its value to help you, not the pain it inflicts. Although your basic instinct may be to react and fight back, you might escalate the problem. Use criticism constructively: *'What can you suggest we do to improve the culture here?'* Don't become upset at their inappropriate style of delivery. *'Where is the evidence that I'm not a team player …?'* Regardless of whether they are correct or wrong don't get upset; ask for advice or just deliver a clever retort (see Strategy 5).

Ultimately, feedback is a guide to help you work out what to do next and adjust your communication skills to obtain the response you require. Listen carefully to others who have wisdom and provide constructive feedback about your actions. You can use professional advice, such as a mentor, to change any of your ineffective, unsuitable behaviours.

Types of feedback:

- Positive feedback: genuine smile, respectful gaze, caring gesture.

  Your response — Acknowledge, thank and store!

- Destructive feedback: sarcasm, mean comments, harsh movements, avoidance.

  Your response — Report, trash or withdraw respect!

- Constructive feedback: valuable information for adjusting your undermining or ineffective behaviours.

  Your response — Respect and utilise truth, regardless of delivery!

Communication tips

Effective listening

Some people hear without absorbing anything — advertising research shows the average attention span is about 22 seconds — but you need to use effective listening skills to survive a bullying situation. These skills help you understand the other person's perspective and work out why they relate in a certain manner. Once you understand, you can communicate more clearly and create a respectful resolution.

Understand the other person

The American Indians suggest walking in a person's moccasins for a while to understand why they behave the way they do. Whether your bully, manager or colleague wears high heels, attends to a smokers' group or belongs to the boys' club, it is useful to understand how they think and feel. Then you can work out how to deal with them.

EXERCISE

The 'empty chair technique' is a simple way to develop understanding yourself and another person, but do it with your therapist or a good friend. Place two chairs opposite each other. Imagine that the bully, target or manager is sitting in the empty chair opposite you. Tell them how you feel about their behaviours. When you have said enough, change places and become them. Then reply. When you have said enough in their role, change chairs and return to your role. Keep doing this until neither can contribute anymore. If you find it difficult to fully express yourself, your coach can guess both parties' thoughts and feelings and, like an actor, express them more clearly.

Discuss what you have discovered. Why did the person behave that way and how do they feel about you? You may be surprised at how much you unconsciously know about this person. Then you can work out appropriate strategies for resolving the conflict.

Build rapport

Rapport is the key to building supportive, intimate and healing connections with others. You build rapport by sharing thoughts and feelings, interests and activities. Just imagine that everyone else in your department, section or tribe is on the other side of a suspension bridge or tightrope. You have to cross over to join them. Don't look down while you are crossing or focus on your stressful feelings, concentrate instead on looking ahead to connect with them. People who have rapport are more likely to understand each other's thoughts and feelings and work together.

Gender differences

Men and women have different biological structures and cultural conditionings so they communicate differently. Despite their differences, both sexes can improve their communication skills by saying what they think, feel and want. This will help you to deal more appropriately with a bully, target, colleague, manager or anyone else.

You need to work out the appropriate communication style for your listener: the female story-telling (process orientated) approach or the male bottom line (goal-oriented) approach. Beware that many people still cannot handle assertive women. You will need to decide whether these skills are safe, suitable or risky. When in doubt, stay neutral and stick to the facts. Understanding the differences can improve your communication style. Here is a sample.

Women are gatherers. They focus upon relationships and ...

- connect and create rapport
- work together and share the credit: '*We did ...*'
- praise each another
- try to resolve differences
- conduct two-faced friendships —frenemies — abandon mates when threatened
- focus on detail

- deal with several issues simultaneously
- release tension by sharing their feelings but minimise their distress
- hope others notice their plight and rescue them.

Communication tips for women:

• Use confident, stronger body language.

• Speak clearly, slowly and emphasise important words.

• Use 'I' to express your feelings, thoughts and achievements.

• Show feelings, if safe to do so.

• Employ action words to confront, compete or request support.

• Don't guess or assume the other person's thoughts — ask them.

• Use chitchat to widen your networks.

• Support your women colleagues: '*Kylie, Jane, Chris and I feel that ...*'

Men are hunters. They focus upon the task to ...

- display their achievements to increase their status
- compete while socialising
- win an argument, not resolve it
- make a point and expect to be heard
- stick by their mates
- focus on one subject at a time
- deal with the basic facts
- claim credit wherever possible
- make major decisions without consulting others.

Communication tips for men

- Use nonthreatening body language, especially with women and younger employees.
- Unclench your jaw, move your facial muscles to show your emotions.
- Use active listening skills to get all the information.
- Show respect and acknowledge the other's story.

- Give and receive feedback.
- Build rapport and share empathy.
- Create connections to work together: *'We did …'*
- Give more credit, especially outside the boy's club.
- Use effective conflict resolution skills.
- Practise social conversation to extend your networks.

Strategy 4 in brief

Developing effective, assertive communication tools is a major strategy in the challenge to empower yourself and others. Communication skills create a simple recipe, which when practised properly enhance your ability to connect with others and obtain their support. It also reduces negative energies between yourself and difficult people. These skills help you appear confident, which increases the respect you give to yourself and receive from others, and they also make the recipient accountable to you. You soon find out who cares for you and will help, and those who don't care about you. The paradox is that when you use effective verbal and nonverbal communication skills to respect yourself and expect others to do likewise, they respect you more.

CHAPTER SIX

Strategy 5: Protect and empower yourself

66After Gwen's family business was sold, she worked part-time for a new store that required her business expertise. The owner targeted Travis, another employee. Gwen said: 'It was a constant battle between me, Travis and the boss.' The owner attacked her for protecting Travis and demanded her allegiance. 'I don't want to become involved with your petty nonsense,' Gwen said, winning that round. He screamed and criticised other staff. He created rivalry by going behind their backs and checking up on others. They became upset, lost their cool and left. Gwen wondered why her boss couldn't make the connection. Each new staff member required training and time to settle into their new job. When she was angry, she wrote letters to him or confronted him: 'Don't talk to me like that'. She slammed down the phone when he was rude. She dealt with the bullying by brushing it off. She knew he needed her but she didn't need his job. When she threatened to leave, he convinced her to stay. I asked how she found the courage to confront him. Gwen said: 'My life experiences and maturity helped me become more assertive. I married later in life to a difficult man and was often forced to challenge him. When I confronted this bully, I was confident and meant what I said.'99

When speaking to an audience about dealing with bullying I often say: 'I was brought up to believe that if you're nice to people, they'll be nice to you.' I ask for a show of hands to see if anyone else was brought up like me. Generally, about half of the audience volunteer. I wonder whether the remainder are shy or weren't brought up like me. Then I say, 'This is ridiculous. About 5% of the population are psychotic, psychopathic, drug or alcohol addicted, about 15% are neurotic, many people still treat women, homosexuals, different races or cultures, the unemployed and mentally ill differently anyway and the rest of us might be just having a bad day. It could be you or me. It doesn't matter how nice you are, someone might be mean to you.' This usually guaranteesa healthy laugh!

Human beings go into survival mode when they are feeling threatened. If you show signs of fear, panic, anger or hurt you catapult the other person's survival instinct into action. They fight or become defensive, like an animal guarding their territory. Sometimes it does not matter how nice you are, if you are dealing with stressed-out employees or sociopaths, they can harass, attack or backstab. If you stand up for your rights and fight back, you lose power and they win. When nothing you do to obtain respect makes a difference, sometimes you need to block people from using difficult or nasty behaviours against you.

Imagine if someone stood on your toes. You would tell them to get off very quickly because it hurts. You could use a similar mental approach with difficult people. You do not want them stepping on your emotional toes. You need to build clear boundaries, like wearing protective body armour to block their psychological bullets. Alternatively, you could visualise yourself plotting a course through a minefield, or around fragile coral at the Great Barrier Reef, or safe in a soundproof room while they yell outside.

You need to maintain your power, not donate it to others. When you block toxic vibes, you protect yourself. As you modify their perceptions, you are less likely to be attacked because you become less threatening. Then others are more likely to respect you. There are lots of empowering tools in this chapter to help you deal more effectively with all types of unkind, dismissive, challenging people and block their power.

Find your inner power

Some time ago we celebrated a friend's 60th birthday. When she arrived at the restaurant she was surprised but thrilled to see her son, her twin sister and Bud, her twin's partner. After lunch, it was time to settle the account. Bud, a wealthy lawyer, divided the bill so that everyone paid for the twins, including my friend's financially struggling son. But I didn't see why we should pay for Bud's partner. No-one spoke. I waited quietly, fuming inside.
I was still recovering from the fact that Bud hadn't offered to pay for an extra bottle of wine. Then something happened inside of me. It was as though every gear in my body was being bypassed until I got to the tenth gear. Throwing my entire conditioning aside, I found the power to say politely to the wealthy lawyer that that wasn't our deal. We had organised to pay for our single friend, not his partner who was his responsibility. (I doubt he felt embarrassed.)

Like the lion in the Wizard of Oz, find the courage to search deep inside yourself and find your inner power to handle difficult or nasty people. Remind yourself: 'I can do it'. The bully shield on the cover of my first book inspired many people, so you can visualise yourself wearing a total body armour as a shield and blocking the bully's abuse, or wearing a bulletproof jacket that repels all their negative vibes they are transmitting to penetrate your identity.

Power surges

Have you ever come home, tired and exhausted? The phone rang and a friend invited you out for a chat or a movie. Suddenly you felt a power surge. After a quick spruce up, off you went, suddenly energised. Maybe you can recall other times when you felt your energy level kick in and you received a power surge.

REFLECTIVE MOMENT

Think about what power means: guts, courage, bravery, taking a risk. Perhaps you recall people whose stories inspired you, a family member or someone you've read about. Remember some of your own previous power surges; perhaps they saved the day at an examination, a wedding day, a job interview, or when you were playing a game.

How can you create your own power surges to protect yourself? What would you need to do? Imagine using your power to confront someone: tell them how you think and feel, monitor their reaction and then reflect back if they reveal a lack of respect for you.

Confrontation tools

Bill captains a cruise ship and loves the sea so much that he lives on his own boat. The ship's owner bullies everyone, including his own daughter, whom Bill has seen cower in the corner, feeling nauseous before facing her abusive father. Bill doesn't have a problem as he can easily find another job. When his boss yells, he confronts him and says: 'I don't like the way you are treating me. Are you trying to get rid of me or do you want me to stay and work for you?' The boss replies in the affirmative, and Bill says: 'Then stop bullying me and make this ship a safe, pleasant, respectful environment.'

The simplest step in managing other employees is to have a direct chat with them or approach their manager, provided it's safe. If you feel too distressed to manage this process alone, find someone suitable to facilitate this discussion. Always remember to document any relevant interaction, such as confirm by email. Remember to manage your emotions and respect others' feelings; try to collaborate to find a solution. Later on, if you have been forced to leave work, these skills will also help you deal with lawyers, medico-legal professionals, insurance companies and others.

- Find the appropriate time and place to discuss the issue.
- Decide whether it is wiser to confront them alone or using witnesses.

- Begin by using their name, a pleasant smile and strong eye contact while remaining calm and respectful. For example: *'John, we have a problem, can we discuss it?' 'Mary, I know you're frustrated, and I respect your opinion, but can I explain my position?'*

- Use assertive verbal skills skills when to focus on describing inappropriate words and behaviours, such as, *'I believe there's too much micro-management in this department.'* Give concrete examples and describe the unproductive results.

- Stay on track and remain task-focused, firm and persistent. Don't let them distract you with shouting, swearing, name-calling, false accusations, faulty interpretations, inappropriate assigning blame, changing the subject, jokes, playing manipulative games or switching to a martyr role.

- Don't sabotage yourself by asking them why they are behaving in this manner. Most people, including bullies, don't know the true reason and even if they did, they would not tell you.

- If an employee explodes when threatened, leave the room and say: *'I'll return when the atmosphere is pleasant again.'* Alternatively, wait for his anger to defuse, like waiting for a child to finish their tantrum.

- Express your desire to resolve your differences together: *'How can we resolve this?'* If the feedback is positive, discuss what needs to change to create safe workplace. If negative, then reflect back; for example: *'Thank you for your feedback, it's clear that my dedication to this job is not appreciated here'*, and then consider the available future options.

Sample confrontations

Describe the current situation:

- *'It seems that whenever I make a suggestion you become defensive, ignore me and listen to others.'*

- *'I cannot see any valid reason for your dismissive, micro-managing, angry or abusive behaviours.'*

- *'I need to talk to you about what happened today when they excluded/gossiped/laughed/spread rumours about me.'*

Ask questions to regain power:

- *'I know we had a difference of opinion some time ago. Is it still upsetting you, as you seem to have changed your attitude towards me?'*
- *'I am aware that you have been speaking about me to others, what are your concerns about me?'*
- *'I told everyone to work together. Why isn't this happening among the team?'*

Describe how the situation affects you; wait silently for feedback:

- *'I'm having a great deal of difficulty handling your anger and can't concentrate for hours afterwards.'*
- *'I am confused when everyone leaves me out of important events.'*
- *'I'm upset that I don't receive the same rewards/shifts/promotion/greeting as everyone else.'*

Acknowledge their fears, frustrations and perceptions:

- *'I appreciate you sharing your point of view.'*
- *'Times are tough and we have to work together, but if this mistake goes unreported, everyone loses.'*
- *'I realise that you're angry with me, but I'm paid to provide professional feedback and suggestions to improve this company so we call benefit.'*

Disarm your bully by agreeing with something:

- *'I agree that I did that wrong ... However, according to the law of averages, everyone makes mistakes, and therefore one mistake shouldn't constitute a sacking offence, I just require constructive feedback to improve.'*
- *'I'm sorry, I was going to do that but I ran out of time.'*

- *'I had a good working relationship with the previous manager; it's hard to adapt to your expectations without knowing exactly what you want from me, unless you intend to change this company but automatically undermine long-term employees.'*

Once the bully is listening, explain yourself, tactfully and assertively:

- *'I'd like to explain why I'm feeling annoyed ...'*
- *'I'm feeling upset because you exclude me from important meetings and emails.'*
- *'I can't concentrate because I can't handle your swearing and invading my space.'*

Ask for what you want; negotiate the options:

- *'What can we do to settle this dispute?'*
- *'I would like you to stop commenting about my figure/love life/sexual needs or I'll take action.'*
- *'I'd like to be treated with the same respect you give to your clients.'*

If they continue manipulating:

- *'Is there anything else we can do to resolve this dispute?'*
- *'I don't find your feedback is constructive or productive for the company.'*
- *'I feel that you're hiding your real agenda.'*

If you can't find a resolution, end the conversation and walk away calmly:

- *'Well I'm sorry we can't resolve this. We have to agree to disagree.'*
- *'You seem more interested in sparring than resolving this issue.'*
- *'I think we need help from others to resolve this.'*

Mean words

They lose their power if you don't cower. (Solomon, 2002)

Social banter is common among tribal networks of close friends, family and workmates. It is accepted as a normal part of sharing fun and social-ising. Words your mother would never allow you to use are now part of everyday speech, such as the 'f' word. When you block bantering skilfully, you demonstrate your inner strength and self-worth. This enables others to respect you. If you are sensitive and overreact, it does not take much for banter to move into a malevolent direction and become abusive.

Although teasing has local fashions, there are common trends. Nobody likes to be teased about being stupid, different, incompetent or excluded. Some nasty expressions never change, such as the slang words for homosexuals, migrants or prostitutes. Sometimes words have a different impact, depending on who says it and where it is being said. Thus being told that you are a bloody idiot by a friend is very different to hearing it from your boss. It is worthwhile trying to check out whether the bully wanted to hurt you or whether these words are part of their normal, everyday vocabulary.

The amount of damage depends on the value that you and colleagues attaches to it. Thus if you are concerned about preserving your status and career, some words can be threatening; they hit your sensitive spots and may invite public embarrassment. Your reaction to an exploratory tease allows bullies to identify your level of vulnerability. They store this away for future reference and use them later as target practice against you. Note that very confident people, or those with 'normal, healthy person-alities' can also become vulnerable with constant verbal harassment.

Martial arts

> Mark wasted a lot of energy fighting and challenging unfair prac-tices. Now he says: 'I'm sorry, I see where you're coming from.' Inside he says: 'Bloody idiot'. He's changed. Now he works to live, not lives to work.

Most types of martial arts are basically self-defence programs, which also build self-esteem, reduce emotional tension and alter body language. They facilitate a 'Don't mess with me' look, rather like a football coach, gym instructor or Grade 3 teacher. When a martial arts expert is attacked, they use their assailant's power against them to block and disempower them. Martial arts are essential training for victims of sexual abuse, physical assault and some school bullying targets. Whether or not you undertake training, you can still use the basic concepts to defuse the bully–target game instead of reacting, losing power and retaliating, escalating the game and losing your power. This can apply to mean bullies who are unaware of the impact of their behaviours, serial bullies or psychopaths (see Field, *Bully Blocking at Work*, 2010, for types of bullies).

Powerhand exercise

> Debbie wrote to me after her exit interview: 'I didn't tape it, but I said a few things that needed to be said. The bully had the gob-smacked and stunned look more than once.'

This is my simple martial arts exercise, the core of dealing with bullying. It is explained in detail in my first two books; it is a metaphor for dealing with bullies and involves two simple processes.

1. Block their power

In the first cartoon, A is pushing B. Their power matches each other's. In the second cartoon A has decided not to push, but tells B to push as hard as they did before. This is impossible as there is nothing to push against. In the third cartoon, B begins to fall towards A and stops. B realises he has lost power and pulls himself back to an upright position. When you ask B why he stopped pushing, he will say that you were not pushing back or your hands went floppy. If you don't push, he loses his power to push you back. If he had kept on pushing, he would lose his balance and fall on top of you. When you stop giving power to the bully, they have less power to abuse or attack.

2. The dumbstruck look

The second process occurs when you take away the bully's power and observe their reaction. Their mouth may drop open, their eyes widen as though stunned and they back off. They look like a fish that has been knocked on the head. This look of disbelief says: *'I don't understand what's happened. I'm giving up; this is a waste of time.'* The bully may laugh oddly, grimace, or seem stuck for words. They feel embarrassed although they may not realise what has happened, just that they feel odd, confused or strange. They may slink off feeling foolish.

By blocking their attack and taking away their power to hurt, you have embarrassed them. Nobody likes to feel embarrassed, not even bullies, especially in front of colleagues. The fear of further embarrassment, witnessed or publicised by peers, acts like an electric shock to stop bullies repeating behaviours that boomerang back on them. However, you don't want to threaten them, you just want them to stop, look stunned and leave you alone. If it is hard to be optimistic, try to be more observant and look for subtle changes in their behaviour; hopefully you will observe physical signs of the dumbstruck look!.

Verbal bully blockers

Retorts or comebacks are simple verbal tricks to help you manage difficult encounters. You just block a verbal punch by being neutral and letting it bounce off you. You don't show your feelings or donate your power to others. Besides, it is nobody's business what you feel inside so don't show it to them.

The secret is to respond sensibly instead of reacting with frustration. Using the powerhand exercise as a metaphor, a neutral retort boomerangs back onto the other person while your power to embarrass them creates a strong invisible barrier, which they are compelled to respect. You could imagine that you are recycling their verbal garbage into a retort or politically correct zinger, or taking the sting out of their tease.

There are lots of bully blockers, and I am including some emergency zingers when nothing else will do. You will find an extensive list here, but there are many others, which you can borrow from movies, friends and everyday life (see my book *Bully Blocking*, Field, 2007). You need to work out what is comfortable, effective and suits your situation. It is useful to write them down and practise them until they pop out automatically at the right moment. You may even say something quite different, once you understand the basic principle. You can mix and match retorts, using simple or complex combinations.

Make sure that you use good communication skills, firm eye contact, upright body language and a strong, clear voice. You need to maintain your blank look, especially when they look surprised. It might be funny but you are not allowed to smile, unless they are out of sight. Just like keeping a packet of tissues handy, plan some easy retorts and have them ready. As bullies are not very creative, once you have used a few good retorts, they will find it harder to reply without risking future embarrassment.

Gentle replies

Be polite

Dame Edna Everage (Barry Humphries) is a great performer, and before she skewers someone in the audience, she softens her blow by saying: *'I mean this in a loving, caring sort of way.'* Thus an example may be:

- *'Is denigrating our staff a new motivation technique?'*
- *'I'd like to agree with you but I view this situation differently.'*

- *'Would you like to hear everyone else's opinion, or can we leave now and you can email us your instructions?'*
- *'Although I respect what you say, I don't agree and will record my opinion.'*
- *'I'll return when you're less angry.'*
- *'I wouldn't say she is a bitch but others would differ.'*
- *'As stress affects my memory you will understand that I need to record this conversation.'*

Be cheeky — use chutzpah

Jewish people have dealt with bullies and persecution for thousands of years. Although Hebrew is the language of Israel and prayer, Yiddish is their international language of survival. 'Chutzpah' is a Yiddish word implying cheek, cunning or daring, thus it is chutzpah to ask for a discount in set price store.

- Ask the bully: *'What can I do to stop you constantly harassing me?'*
- Tell the bully: *'If you need to bully, find a punching bag and leave my employees alone.'*
- Ask workmate: *'What can we do to stop her from bullying others?'* Or: *'What can we do to reduce the toxic tension around here?'*
- Ask your employer: *'Why do you allow some people to bully others when it sabotages performance and productivity?'*

Make a joke

The senior partner in a large law firm believes it is safer to create a fun, bantering environment. He reframes the bullying behaviours of other lawyers by creating jokes to defuse the situation.

- *'Don't ask Rob to work with Maria because he always yells at her and then she goes through a box of tissues, ha ha.'*
- *'You private school boys can't deal with state school fellows, so we'll give this case to Jeremy.'*
- *'You get the bully of the year award.'*
- *'Bill, you've had too many coffees and you're becoming aggressive.'*

- *'Damn it Bryce, I bet John a few dollars that you wouldn't bully the girls until after lunch and now I've lost.'*
- *'When are you planning to micromanage me this week?'*
- *'It's not that he is mean, he didn't learn how to respect others while he was growing up.'*
- *'I wonder whom you will bully if I leave?'*
- *'That used to be a good tease, but it is so dated now!'*
- *'That's off the Richter scale for insensitivity!'*

Show gratitude

Sometimes we learn more from our mistakes than from our successes. Be grateful that you are learning how to deal with mean, difficult, incompetent, lazy or poor communicators.

- Bully: *'That's useless.'*
  Reply: *'Thank you for the truth.'*
- Bully: *'You're stupid.'*
  Reply: *'Is this my performance review?'*
- Bully: *'You're a real f…ing bastard.'*
  Reply: *'Thanks for your interest in my the family history.'*
- Bully: *'Hey wog/chink/nigger/dago …'*
  Reply: *'It's nice that you can spare the time to talk to migrants.'*

Baffle and fluff

The late Luciano Pavarotti was challenged about the amount of tax he paid. *'I don't feel like a tax evader,'* he said. *'I simply misinterpreted an unclear law.'* Language can be precise or vague, constructive or negative. When you feel unsure, try some baffle and fluff. It is politically correct, sounds right but has little meaning.

- *'I didn't realise that I should have done XYZ. Clearly I misinterpreted your instructions.'*
- *'That's very interesting. I'll get back to you on that.'*
- *'I'll discuss that with my mentor.'*

- *'You have made your attitude clear.'*
- *'I'll see what I can do for you.'*

Tougher replies

I often meet parents who tell their children not to swear. Therefore when these children are the targets of swearing at school they are powerless, as they are not allowed to report it. Nothing much seems to change at work, where targets can encounter a barrage of words that most employees would never use in front of their friends or boss. The fact is that some people are exposed to a combination of disgusting, rude and hurtful words.

The clue is not to shrivel or escalate the language but to use simple strategies to block these nasty words with some strong retorts. Thus, although you may find some of the words below offensive, the retorts are designed to equip you in managing them, not succumbing to them. I would like to suggest that you only use these responses if they are suitable for your work environment and if you are comfortable with using the language. If not, there are lots of other more generic examples to use at the end of this chapter.

Confronting criticism

Bullies know how to push your sensitive spots. Don't become upset and react. Ask for clarification, reframe and eyeball them.

Direct attack: *'That's a bloody stupid thing to do.'*

Reply: *'I hear what you say. What do you suggest I do?'*

Or: *'That's interesting, where's your evidence?'*

Exclusion: *'You don't belong here.'*

Reply: *'Please explain exactly what you mean?'*

Or: *'Quite true, I can't understand why I am still working where I'm not valued?'*

Denigrate: *'You're a troublemaker.'*

Reply: *'I'm employed to maintain a high professional standard so you should be pleased that I'm doing what I am paid to do.'*

Challenge

When the bully is unusually quiet …

Reply: *'Bob, you haven't teased me this week, is anything wrong?'*

To the office pervert …

Reply: *'If you're undressing me mentally, give me a perfect body. Otherwise it's a waste of time seeing it.'*

Be assertive

- *'Stop it.'*
- *'Wait a moment, this isn't fair.'*
- *'I can't believe that you're saying this.'*
- *'I don't like what's happening right now.'*
- *'I find that really offensive.'*
- *'Ouch, that hurts.'*
- *'I listened to you, Now can you listen to me?'*
- *'Stop barking, I heard you the first time.'*

Clarify

- *'Are you aware that I don't like your disrespectful behaviours towards me?'*
- *'What exactly do you mean by …?'*
- *'What do you feel when you describe want to achieve by telling me about your sex life to me?'*
- *'Why do you believe that I am doing this wrong …?'*

Use the broken record technique

- *'I cannot handle this extra assignment. I need to complete my set duties first.'* (Repeat)
- *'I don't want to give that to you …'* (Repeat)
- *'Can you answer my question …?'* (Repeat)
- *'Have you forgotten that I told you that I can't complete my work while you are yelling at me?'*

Telling the truth

> *Susan is a leading management consultant. Once, while speaking with a CEO, she was feeling threatened. 'Can we stop for a minute?' she asked. 'Would you be open to feedback about something I am experiencing?' He nodded. 'Are you trying to bully me?' she asked. The CEO stopped, 'What do you mean?' Susan replied, 'You're being forceful and it felt like intimidation.' He appeared shocked but apologised.*

There is an incredible cultural pressure on most people to be nice, not honest, so others may be surprised when you utter the truth. They may think you are joking or bluffing, and back off feeling stunned and confused. Nobody wants to be identified as a bully, because it implies a fundamental character flaw. If you find it impossible to disguise your feelings, then be honest and share your feelings.

- *'I'm planning my week. How often do you intend to harass my staff?'*
- *'I have an allergy to unproductive stress.'*
- *'You new guys have to be careful you don't bully the oldies.'*
- *'I'm offended by the way you roll your eyes at my workmates.'*
- *'I don't like you tarnishing my good name; I need to use it as it is.'*

Courtroom blockers

For occasions when you are in a more formal legal situation such as a mediation, conciliation or courtroom:

- *'I can't remember the words she used but I won't forget the location and the bystanders' embarrassment.'*
- *'That's a long time ago.'*
- *'It may be in my notes.'*
- *'The experts say that bullying can affect my memory.'*
- *'I remember my fear and humiliation, not the details.'*
- *'My records show that I actually allowed him to bully me on many occasions, not just one.'*
- *'Nothing else caused my injuries, I was fine before it started.'*
- *'My previous performance review was excellent, why wasn't that taken into consideration?'*

Everyday retorts

Agree or acknowledge:

Bully: *'You are a real loser.'*

Reply: *'Sure, I'm a paid up member of our local loser's group.'*

Bully: *You're an idiot.*

Reply: *'And I'm going for my licence soon.'* Or: *'I could include more brain food in my diet.'*

Bully: *'Hey shortie ...'*

Reply: *'Yes, it's genetic.'*

Bully: *'Gee you're fat ...'*

Reply: *'I know; it's a real handicap.'* Or: *'I love food. Thanks, I thought I was enormous.'*

Bully: *'You're a wanker ...'*

Reply: *'I've got nothing else to do in my spare time.'* Or: *'It's a male thing.'*

Bully: *'You're a dickhead.'*

Reply: *'Takes one to know one mate.'*

Suck-up stuff

Bully: *'You're not pulling your weight!'*

Reply: *'Would you like me to put on another 10 kilos?* Or: *'Maybe human resources placed me in the wrong job.'*

Bully: *'You're not a team player.'*

Reply: *'Teams depend upon good leadership, any suggestions?'*

Bully: *'You're sloppy!'*

Reply: *'Yeah, whatever.'* Or: *'No, I'm still working at it.'*

Disagree

Bully: *'You're stupid.'*

Reply: *'No I was stupid on Monday; Tuesday I was a moron, Wednesday a nutcase and today I'm a dickhead for wasting my time talking to you instead of working.'*

Bully: *'Suck my dick.'*

Reply: *'Sorry I don't have a magnifying glass with me.'*

Bully: *'You're a motherfucker.'*

Reply: *'Nah, that's my dad's job.'*

Bully: *'Shut up.'*

Reply: *'I'm busy right now.'* Or: *'My brain works better when I verbalise.'*

Be apologetic

Bully: *'You're not allowed in here!'* Or: *'What are you doing here?'*

Reply: *'I'm sorry but I left my pass at home.'*

Bully: *'You're a fuckwit.'*

Reply: *'Yes. It's the family curse.'* Or: *'That is what sex does to a person.'*

Change direction

Bully: *'You clumsy fool.'*

Reply: *'They don't call me fumble fingers for nothing.'*

Bully: *'Fuck your mother ...'*

Reply: *'Let's keep family politics out of work.'*

Bully: *'That was stupid.'*

Reply: *'Well my brother has three degrees, I'm not as smart.'*

Bully: *'You've got no idea how to do it.'*

Reply: *'It's sad but I'm the victim of family genetics.'*

Bully: *'Did you have sex with your date?'*

Reply: *'I'll give you zero out of ten for tact.'*

Ask questions

Bully: *'You're an arsehole.'*

Reply: *'Who told you?'*

Bully: *'You're a bitch.'*

Reply: *'Shall I go back to my kennel now or later?'*

Bully: *'Hey you …'*

Reply: *'Do you mind telling me why you always look at me up and down like that?'*

Bully: *'You're a shit.'*

Reply: *'Do you want to see the rest of my blemishes? It won't take long.'*

Clarify

Bully: *'Hey homo …'*

Reply: *'Where's your evidence?'* Or: *'Isn't it better to be clear about one's sexuality rather than confused?'*

Bully: *'Do you want to hear a blonde joke?'*

Reply: *'Is it a natural or tinted blonde joke?'*

Bully: *'Hey dickhead …'*

Reply: *'Are you talking about my penis or my brain?'*

Negotiate

Bully: *'Get lost …'*

Reply: *'If you stop harassing me, I won't put plan B into action and email our board members.'*

Bully: *'Hey you big fart …'*

Reply: *'I don't like being bullied, so can we discuss my options?'*

Bully to Irish employee: *'Do you want to hear an Irish joke?'*

Reply: *'I love Irish jokes. If I haven't heard it before, I'll give you a bottle of my favourite whisky; if I have, then you give me a bottle.'*

Ask for feedback

Bully: *'Get out of here …'*

Reply: *'How exactly do I aggravate you?'*

Bully: *'Hey you …'*

Reply: *'What do you feel when you snigger and gossip when your target walks past? What do they think they are feeling?'*

Bully: *'That is fucking useless.'*

Reply: *'Do I file that under F or U?'*

Get in first

You can criticise or make a joke about yourself, to take away the bully's power.

- *'I may be middle-aged but I can't see what's funny about bullying someone.'*
- *'I've been here too long, what's going on here now?'*

Take action

Bully: *'She's got a great bum.'*

Reply: *'The police call that harassment.'*

Bully: *'Hey move over …'*

Reply: *'If you keep knocking me, I'll take out an intervention order against you.'*

Variety of replies

Bully: *'Hey dickhead.'*

Reply: *'Can you photograph it for the Guinness Book of Records?'* Or: *'Is it better to be a dickhead or an arsehole?'* Or: *'And I can use them simultaneously, do you know anyone else who can?'*

Bully: *'You're the weakest link.'*

Reply: *'You're repeating yourself. Can you use something else tomorrow?'* Or: *'Are you saying I'm made of gold, silver or platinum?'* Or: *'I believe in good management, not reality television.'*

Generic replies

- *'And?'*
- *'Right.'*
- *'Fancy that.'*
- *'Really, I heard you.'*
- *'Life's a bitch.'*
- *'Thanks for the feedback.'*
- *'You've an interesting way of viewing things; I'll try that later (in my next life).'*
- *'Have you thought about wording that differently?'*
- *'Whatever.'*
- *'Sure thing.'*
- *'I heard you.'*

Emergency replies

Zapper: A zapper is a sudden blast that can stun its adversary, like a pressure pack.

- *'I'm not always this stupid.'*
- *'How do you know I am …?'*

- *'You've caught me on a bad day. I don't always do …'*
- *'You've drawn the short straw with me. But at least I try harder than many others do.'*
- *'How much are you enjoying seeing me stressed by your micromanagement?'*
- *'Why can't you be direct and tell me what you dislike about me or what I do to make you laugh?'*

Zinger: A zinger is a sarcastic one-liner. It can give you a good laugh with friends in private and function as an emotional release. But remember — it can advertise your frustration and invite further retaliation, but if you are extremely desperate, use a bland face, strong eye contact, neutral body language and clear voice.

- *'Silence may be golden, but not from you.'*
- *'How can you run a profitable business when you reward incompetence?'*
- *'Cough, cough, I'm allergic to bullshit.'*
- *'I don't know what your problem is, but I bet it's hard to pronounce.'*
- *'I'm hoping that one day you'll tell me something really useful.'*
- *'Thanks for the ineffectual feedback.'*
- *'You look as though you enjoy bullying, it probably takes away attention from your other problems.'*
- *'Have you mistaken me for someone who cares about what you think?'*
- *'Are you taking a new brand of idiot tablets?'*
- *'When did you have your personality bypass?'*
- *'Do I have stupid written across my head? Don't give me that rubbish?'*
- *'Here's a dollar. Ring someone who cares.'*
- *'Who's on your bullying agenda for next week?'*
- *'Are you always mean, or do you practise especially for our team?'*
- *'Have you been genetically modified?'*
- *'They are off the Richter scale for stupidity/laziness/corruption.'*

Strategy 5 in brief

Like a firefighter's uniform, managing abrasive, difficult or vicious people is an essential strategy for any workplace. Once you have managed to block bullies, everyone will respect you and then you can work on building your career. The clue is to remain calm, prepare your strategies, and take action to block. If you reveal your anger or fear, then they will feel threatened and escalate their attack, trying to destroy you rather than themselves.

CHAPTER SEVEN

Strategy 6:
Use your support network

❝*I was a competent credit controller at the union for years. In January, management sneakily appointed someone above me. I had seen their destructive bullying previously and realised I was next. During February I tried to look for other work, but couldn't pull it together. My mind went blank at the job interview. By May I left, too sick to function. Despite many other cases, my employers denied the bullying. For two years I became a daily 'doona diver'. Eventually, my compensation case was resolved. The real validation came when conciliation forced my employer's insurers to fund my aromatherapy retraining. Looking back, I was alone at work and felt as if I didn't exist. My work friends had left or were too scared to support me. But I had an effective support network — my husband, a lawyer, a general practitioner, the organisational psychologist who investigated the work culture and colleagues who were bullied previously. One wrote a book about workplace bullying, which legitimised my awful experiences. Without their support, understanding and knowledge, I would have broken down. They supported me through this horrible time at work.* **❞**

Everyone needs a social support network to survive. Your networks protect you from the stresses of coping with life's ups and downs. They validate your negative experiences by enabling you to share them with empathic listeners and create the opportunities for valuable feedback. They maintain your emotional resilience and behave like a stress barrier. Ultimately, they reduce the devastating symptoms of stress, depression and trauma.

There may be times in your life when you want to be alone, deal with your stressful feelings and find the energy to regenerate. But when dealing with workplace bullying, it is extremely unwise to isolate yourself from supportive, sensible people. You will feel even more alone, frustrated and powerless. Research has shown that you need all the help and social support available. Thus you need to share without burdening others. This involves respecting their needs, but utilising their feedback while maintaining the usual bonds of family and friendships.

Many cultures, from an Italian village to the hill tribes of Vietnam, maintain daily contact with their extended family, as they have done for generations. Unfortunately, with increasing industrialisation and relocation, most people in western societies are infected by an anti-tribal disease that fosters adversarial or absentee relationships, not collaborative ones. Sadly, most people lose regular contact with their extended families and are even more alone when trauma strikes.

Someone to watch over you

Being affected directly or indirectly by workplace bullying may seem a vague, harmless, insidious sort of injury. So although there is value in sharing with friends, colleagues and family, you also need unconditional support and caring from a few significant people, such as your partner, a sibling, a flatmate or best friend.

If you are unable to access help from family or work friends then find someone to mentor you until the bullying matters have resolved. This person may be a coach, therapist, family doctor or minister; alternatively you can develop special bonds with a workmate, neighbour, hairdresser, masseur or even fellow commuters.

Your support team

Generally, people prefer a small circle of close friends and a larger group of acquaintances. When you create effective relationships with family, friends and professionals, you develop your support team. Aim for a variety of people to empower you by creating strong connections with each one. This involves being honest and sharing your stresses with these caring people regularly.

Most friends have an automatic time limit and switch off when overwhelmed with your workplace worries. You don't want to lose a support person because they have been burnt out. It's better to lean a little bit on a number of people rather than burdening one or two with all your difficulties. You still need to remain sociable and spread yourself around like honey.

You may consider different levels of friendship. Your family members or true friends will provide advice, care and emotional intimacy. These deeper levels of sharing are validating and healing. Your social chitchat acquaintances provide support and opportunities to switch off, relax and share some leisure. They can offer tips on dealing with bullying and allow you to release some hurt, confusion and anger.

Socialising for targets and victims is stressful. Chitchat is hard, especially when you are feeling angry, hurt and powerless. If you are in pain, it is difficult to maintain many levels of friendship as you may want to focus on the bullying, while family and friends want to chat about cheerful stuff or share their own difficulties. However, you still need to try.

If you find it hard to be cheerful and socialise, you can still obtain that primitive sense of tribal belonging, acceptance and counteract loneliness by attending regular religious or recreational events, such as the movies, alone or with friends. It is best to avoid people who hurt without intending to, cannot cope with your problems, don't care because of their own issues, or those you cannot trust anymore.

You may find that, apart from a loyal few, many friends and family find it difficult to be constantly supportive over a long period of time. Like others who experience trauma or tragedy, you may be surprised by where your support and caring actually comes. It can surface from the least expected sources. Sometimes people share more with a stranger they meet on their travels than their nearest and dearest. You may obtain extra support from strangers who are less emotionally involved, and who you are less likely to see when it is over. Look for these kind people.

Types of people

Many years ago I had the privilege of sharing a drink of hot chocolate with the late Viktor Frankl, a Holocaust survivor and world-renowned author of *Man's Search for Meaning* (1959). He told me there were only two types of people in the world: nice people and not nice people. Thus you can distinguish between people who care about you and those who don't care.

Because you have limited energies, separate the nice, caring people into two categories: the low maintenance list of easy-to-be-with people and the high maintenance list of emotionally draining people. Instead of hurting their feelings and losing their friendship, tell them that you will make social arrangements when you feel better, or meet them in more superficial surroundings such as shopping centres, sports events. In the meantime, the occasional card, email or phone call, will suffice.

Don't be bullied by your supporters

> Tracey left her job because she was being bullied and found an interesting, well-paying position. To her horror, her next boss was also a bully. She rang her psychologist for another appointment, but her husband bullied her to cancel. Evidently he was more concerned about finances than her emotional wellbeing. Neither had considered asking the psychologist to delay payment, as she had done previously. Sadly, Tracey didn't learn how to confront her new boss and resigned later. Her current job pays less and is far less stimulating.

You need to ensure that everyone you rely upon for support is doing just that, at work and at home. You may need to check out any family and others who are also stressing you and block their behaviours. Otherwise they will hinder your ability to manage your work challenges. You may also need to watch out for those who operate a mental stopwatch and set a time limit on your story, such as six months, and then switch off. They may use the following questions: *'Aren't you over that now?' 'Hasn't that finished yet?'* This too will sabotage your recovery.

Your support network

Once you have worked out your support network you need to involve them regularly. Your list needs to include personal, work and other support networks.

Personal

This group comprises family and friends, including your partner, parents, grandparents, children, siblings, extended family and friends or even neighbours, sports or gym group, regular shopkeepers, hairdresser.

Family

If you live with your family, give them regular updates, such as during your family meetings, and briefly share your feelings. Try to release your distress elsewhere to avoid hurting them. A child at any age will sense a parent's distress, so don't be secretive, simply share what is making you sad, scared or grumpy, otherwise they will blame themselves for stressing you, as children do.

This is a good time to search your family tree and forget old family feuds or differences, to renew phone, email or face-to-face contact with distant cousins, aunts and uncles. Although you will not connect with everyone, some may become supportive and help you through these difficult times.

Family action

- Organise regular family meetings with your partner and children.
- Provide a regular brief up-to-date summary.
- Obtain feedback about the impact on them and how regularly they require an update.
- Spend time every week doing family things, such as a family meal or picnic, and quality time with each one individually, so no-one misses out on your attention.
- Bullying can reduce your sex urge and affect your marital relationship. Find ways to compensate so that your relationship does not break down.

- Bring your partner and children to meet your therapist who can explain your workplace bullying injuries more simply.

- Make a family mission statement about what is important to you and your family. Measure this on a scale of 1 to 10. How important is this nasty job in comparison?

Friends

Friends are strong sources of emotional support, especially while you are dealing with challenges. They provide a listening ear, a different perspective, and constructive feedback on how to manage the situation differently. They may have useful contacts, know the bully's boss, help you find another job, interpret letters and emails, or share weekends away.

If you are a private sort of person who finds it difficult to burden your friends with your problems, remember that we all experience ups and downs. No-one is totally free from stress and trauma. This is your turn for support — another time you can give to them. If you cannot share bad times with friends, then you cannot share a true friendship.

However, don't dump all your problems on them. They may have difficulty coping, burn out and move away. Then you could lose their support when you need it most. Remember that your coach or therapist is trained to deal with your problems, not your friends. It is wise to check what they can cope with. For example: *'I need to rant and rave, can you nod with empathy?' 'How much time can you give me for this?'*

Maintain your friendships

If you confide easily and often with family and friends, tell them that you will may need to repeat and review your bullying story regularly. Ask them to be patient with your obsessing, it is a symptom of workplace bullying trauma (WBT; refer to Field, *Bully Blocking at Work*, 2010) and thus it is healing to release your story. Tell them you don't always require advice, that is the role of your professional support team, just empathic listening.

A reliable car or a well-organised home require regular maintenance. Similarly, you need to maintain your friendships by providing support, empathy, show interest and make them feel special. You need to maintain regular contact, as one-way friendships eventually deteriorate.

- Communicate with a few friends weekly — face-to-face or via phone or email.
- Initiate contact — don't wait for them.
- Meet regularly enough to fulfil both your needs.
- Replace stressful intimate conversations with casual chats — for example, about clothes, food, gardening, movies, sport, hobbies, children, parents.

Support structures at work

This includes colleagues, mates, other employees nearby, the smokers' group, walking group.

You meet all sorts of people at work, including those who are conscientious, shy, handicapped, ambitious, extremely jealous, competitive, controlling or aggressive. Some are friendly and supportive; others take your food from the communal fridge. Others repress or obsess about details, focus upon things unrelated to work, expect others to cover up or clean up for them, or rely upon outdated work practices.

You cannot choose who you work with. The key is to be courteous to everyone — in the lifts, corridors and open plan offices. Smile, greet and say something cordial such as, *'How's your day been so far?' Do you have plans for your weekend?'* Remember that this is a working environment, not a social gathering. You need to be polite and respectful, but build clearer, stronger boundaries than you allow within your social groups.

Working relationships

Work is easier when people are friendly. Socialising creates a cheerful, relaxed environment and fosters effective, collaborative teams. This leads to a more motivated and stimulated work culture, provided there are no exclusive cliques or clubs. Research shows that the social support of work colleagues is extremely important in counteracting the difficulties associated with workplace bullying (Soares, 2004).

Not only do colleagues provide emotional support and empathy, but they understand management difficulties, the work culture and the bullying games. Many have experienced or witnessed bullying elsewhere at work. They can advise you on how to manage your bullying difficulties and provide you with public support. They may be affiliated with powerful networks that spread the word about what is happening and inform management. Bullies are less likely to target people who are fully supported by their work group; they will not welcome any embarrassing publicity associated with bullying.

Find out who is genuinely supportive and who is prepared to be an active bystander, to confront bullies or take group action. Most employees will put their job security first and consider their mortgage and superannuation before your friendship, so value any assistance colleagues offer and understand when they are powerless to help.

- Build your power base with others at work to extend and strengthen your network.

- Use your survival instinct to work out who is trustworthy and to what extent.

- If you feel alienated, make a special effort to be friendly, obtain feedback from friends to change your behaviours, or find others to socialise with.

- Don't automatically trust people because you work together, socialise or share an office.

- Beware of workmates who encourage you to get them but abandon or betray you when they fear being targeted or dismissed.

- Maintain regular contact by email, phone, during lunchtime and after hours.

- Don't get them or yourself into trouble by speaking about difficulties during work hours.

- Keep their contact details at home, in case you are forced to leave and need to contact them.

Other employees

> *Rachel said that everyone is too scared to confront the boss.*
> *Everyone is too well paid and terrified of losing their job.*
> *However, they debrief with one another.*

Although you may feel as though you are the only person managing bullying at your workplace, it is highly likely that bullying has occurred previously and is still occurring elsewhere, if your organisation has ineffective practices to stop it. Speak to others to obtain a bird's eye view of how your workplace manages bullying, to obtain evidence about successful resolutions or horror stories.

It is useful to get advice from those who have experienced, witnessed or managed bullying blow-ups, even though each person may perceive it differently. The target with a financially secure partner may find it easier to ignore, confront or leave. Those employees with serious financial responsibilities or limited job opportunities feel compelled to remain. The bully with major family problems may require a different approach to the serial bully who is covering up major relating difficulties. Bullying in one part of the company may need to be managed differently to another section.

Bystander action

Nowadays we are becoming more aware of the value of bystander interventions, as school students stop bullying very quickly if their peers intervene. Research demonstrates that many witnesses are injured by bullying; their morale, performance, health and reputation can suffer, thus 20% will leave (Rayner, 1997). Perhaps you can encourage others to become active witnesses. They can:

- confront people who use bullying behaviours, without threatening them.
- create a lobby group to inform their manager, senior management, managing director or board of directors.
- instigate a collective complaint or initiate group legal action.

Human resources

> *Betty said that her human resources manager was worse than her bully. She altered the details of their meeting, failed to accurately report what Betty and her bully had said and didn't investigate their complaints.*

Some human resource departments deal with bullying quickly and effectively. They understand what it involves and have the skills, resources and responsibility to validate, intervene and resolve the power imbalance. However, like some mental health professionals, many human resources personnel have limited training, skills and knowledge. They have little understanding about the financial repercussions of bullying to their organisation and the impact of individual psychological injuries on their workforce and the cost of this damage.

Sometimes they intervene with a sledgehammer, when pliers would be more effective. This occurs when they instigate a major investigation when a small round-table consultation conference or a group restructure would suffice.

As their role is to represent management, not the employee, their goal is to please or placate their employer and reduce any liabilities to the company. Many focus on risk management rather than productivity. I know that many are powerless or ignorant; some suffer bullying themselves or lack the power to reduce bullying.

You need to consult your colleagues about human resources and what they can do to assist. Investigate what they know about workplace bullying. You could educate them by providing more information — for example:

- *'This audit shows the performance and financial damage caused by the bullying.'*
- *'Five people who were bullied out are receiving Workcover now. how much have the insurance premiums increased due to this bully?'*
- *'This list contains my symptoms caused by the bullying.'*

You could add bystanders' symptoms list too. Suggest simple solutions — for example:

- *'All she needs is an apology.'*
- *'Why don't you video them for a few months.'*

Ultimately, you need to assess if they will help, hinder or harm you.

Improve your networking strategies

Networks include strangers, acquaintances, friends and others such as sporting mates who are external to your organisation. Not only is it professionally rewarding to establish wider networks, but you may obtain support and strategies in managing bullying difficulties. If you have powerful external contacts, you may encounter fewer difficulties in managing bullying situations, provided you don't threaten the bully and his support team. Alternatively, networking may help you obtain a better job elsewhere. It may encourage others to speculate why you left, and why your job is being advertised, and this could boomerang back onto your employer. In some industries, the grapevine does influence the job-seeking employment market as potentially excellent employees are wary about applying for positions where bullying is rife.

Other support structures

These include the significant others outside your workplace; for example, professionals, the forums and social web sites on the Internet, unions, police and media.

Significant others

There is a variety of people outside your workplace who can support, help and empower you. This list includes professionals such as lawyers, general practitioners, psychologists, psychiatrists, ministers, telephone helplines and statutory occupational health and safety investigators. You can contact people with influence like your Member of Parliament or the Ombudsman. You might establish a lobby group to help targets.

The internet

> *'Many of us were desperate when first arriving here at Nineveh (a web group) and many of us have weathered the storm and suffered setbacks. But the bottom line is we're making it through and supporting each other. You cannot change what's happened. Now you must move on and fight to regain your strength.'*

I urge you to discover the wonderful world wide web of workplace bullying. You can share your difficulties with others who understand, and obtain information. Although they may live in another state or country, have different working environments and legislation, no country confronts workplace bullying effectively. Around the world, bullying at work is dealt with unfairly and foolishly.

- Investigate academic research, international conferences, professional papers, general information.
- Find appropriate social media sites for sharing personal experiences and advice.
- Google websites with terms like 'workplace bullying', 'mobbing', 'harassment'.
- Investigate government, employer and human rights organisations, academic institutions, unions, psychiatric and psychological sites and media articles.
- Join online self-help groups.

Unions

Your union or professional association is a source of information, support, intervention and legal advice or representation. You should consult them regularly and keep them up to date. They may even know of others being bullied at your workplace. Find out what type of constructive action they can initiate between you and your employer, as well as their previous successes and failures. Some unions provide skilled professional legal advice though you will need to investigate any costs and timeframe.

Beware that many unions do not fully understand workplace bullying and have limited power to reduce it. Don't expect miracles. Be wary of promises they cannot fulfil or those who display a superficial, short-term interest in your welfare. Some are manipulated by bully employers, use your case to promote their own political agendas, build their public profile or attack unethical organisations.

Trial by media

In the past few years, the media has played a significant role in raising public awareness about workplace bullying. The pressured, competitive culture of media encourages journalists to expose many stories. You can contact editors and producers in radio, print, internet or television and send a carefully written press release. Make sure that you don't hurt yourself or someone else in the process. Ultimately, the media becomes the most public and powerful tool in re-educating employers about the evils associated with workplace bullying.

Strategy 7 in brief

Lions are pretty tough animals, but they all follow their leader. They know that they have more to eat if they work together to catch their prey. The resilience demonstrated by Holocaust survivors is due in part to their strong support networks. Likewise, although you will often feel like retreating to a secluded safe place, sometimes you need to obtain personal and professional support, assistance and guidance so that you are not alone in dealing with your workplace stresses. When you use the support of supervisors, peers and subordinates, and incorporate their feedback and encouragement, then you will survive better. You may need some coaching and guidance on how to apply new methods of relating to your team. In fact, when you feel the instinctual (but possibly self-harming) need to fight for justice, listen to your support group — they may suggest a safer, less harmful approach to help you move on.

Conclusion

Before the New Zealand book launch of *Bully Busting* (1999) I spent a few days in the Bay of Islands. I remember sitting close to a warm, open fire, intending to begin my next book for shy children and hoping to ease my pain following the book's traumatic release in Australia. Then I overhead an amazing story about workplace bullying, and I collected more everywhere I went. Had I become more perceptive to what happens in the workplace following the bullying I encountered with my first book? Did the distance from home open my mind? It no longer matters, I had experienced a major revelation.

Since then, an amazing pathway has materialised and my new journey began. However, while writing these books on workplace bullying, I encountered many ups and downs, including a lymphoma, anaemia, countless rejections, as well as many new discoveries. At some stages my life mirrored my clients, without the bullying experiences.

At an age when I should have reached a professional plateau and planning retirement, I am still investigating new areas of workplace bullying, including diagnosis, treatment, prevention and training. My mission has created an unusual but stimulating journey, without clear professional guidelines or boundaries. This approach has enabled me to maintain an open, objective perspective — to learn from everyone and everything.

I owe a deep gratitude to the real experts, those who experienced bullying and trusted me to help them. Hopefully, some of their pain has been validated, as their stories inspired the strategies. Perhaps their experiences will inspire you to initiate your own journey, despite its ups and downs, to build a better life for yourself and your loved ones.

Thus I hope that my years of research and clinical practice will give you more skills, options and strategies to manage bullying. I also invite you to join me in educating, mentoring and managing others so that workplaces become safer, enjoyable and more productive, as I believe that this change is beginning.

However, beware that venturing into the world of workplace bullying in the pursuit of justice may seem obligatory, but it is just an option, which becomes extremely dangerous if you don't take care of health and wellbeing while pursuing that justice.

At any stage of this journey, you need to identify your true goals and values, remind yourself that you only have one life to live and that because it is totally disempowering and painful to live with the injustice of bullying forever, there needs to be a moment when you say: *'Enough is enough! Regardless of what has happened, it is time for me to move on, store my workplace bullying problems away and build a new life — while I can.'*

Evelyn M. Field, FAPS

References

Introduction

Calwell, S., & Johnston, D. (1998). *There's more to life than sex and money.* Melbourne, Australia: Penguin.

Field, E.M. (1999). *Bully busting.* Sydney, Australia: Finch.

Field, E.M. (2007). *Bully blocking.* Sydney, Australia: Finch.

Chapter 1

Crawshaw, L. (2007). *Taming the abrasive manager: How to end unnecessary roughness in the workplace.* San Francisco: Jossey-Bass.

De Vente, W., Kamphuis, J.H., Emmelkamp, P.M.G., & Blonk, R.W.B. (2008). Individual and group cognitive-behavioral treatment for work-related stress complaints and sickness absence: A randomized controlled trial. *Journal of Occupational Health Psychology, 13*(3), 214-231.

Einarsen, S., Hoel, H., Zapf, D., & Cooper C.L. (Eds.) (2011). *Bullying and harassment in the workplace: Developments in theory, research and practice.* Boca Raton, FL: CRC Press.

Eisenberg, N.I., Lieberman, M.D, & Williams, K.D. (2003). Does rejection hurt? An MRI study of social exclusion, *Science, 302,* 290–292.

Field, E.M. (2010a). *Bully blocking at work.* Brisbane, Australia: Australian Academic Press.

Field, E.M. (2010b, June). *Workplace bullying trauma (WBT) – fantasy, fact or the future?* Paper presented to the 7th International Conference on Workplace Bullying and Harassment: Transforming Research: Evidence and Practice, Cardiff, Wales.

Jackson, D., Firtko, A., & Edenborough, M. (2007). Personal resilience as a strategy for surviving and thriving in the face of workplace adversity: A literature review. *Journal of Advanced Nursing, 60*(1),1–9.

Lutgen-Sandvik, P. (2008). Intensive remedial identity work: Responses to workplace bullying trauma and stigmatization. *Organization Articles, 15*(1), 97–119.

O'Moore, M., & Crowley, N. (2011). The clinical effects of workplace bullying: A critical look at personality using SEM. *International Journal of Workplace Health Management, 4*(1), 67–83.

Rayner, C., Howl, H., & Cooper, G. (2002). *Workplace bullying: what we know, who is to blame and what can we do?* London: Taylor and Francis.

Tehrani, N. (2001). *Building a culture of respect.* London & New York: Taylor Francis.

Worksafe. (2009). *Preventing and responding to bullying at work.* Sydney, Australia: Author.

Chapter 2

Bishop, S. (2011, Feb 13). The role of neural pathways, weather we develop and overcome fears, science daily, *Science Daily.*

Davidson, R. (2009). More compassion, less competition. *Monitor on Psychology, 40*(11), 21.

Field, E.M. (2007). *Bully blocking.* Sydney, Australia: Finch.

Koren, G., & Van Umm, S. (2010, September 6). Link between chronic stress and heart attack: Hair provides proof. *Medical News Today.*

Gordon, I. (2003, August). Shark expert. *The Age, Sunday Life.*

Lieberman, M.D., Jarcho, J.M., Berman, S., Naliboff, B.D., Suyenobu, B.Y., Mandelkern, M., & Mayer, E.A. (2004). The neural correlates of placebo effects: A disruption account. *Neuroimage, 22*(1), 447–455.

Chapter 3

Crawshaw, L. (2007). *Taming the abrasive manager: How to end unnecessary roughness in the workplace.* San Francisco: Jossey-Bass.

Djurkovic, N., McCormack, D., & Casimir, G. (2006). Neuroticism and the psychosomatic model of workplace bullying. *Journal of Managerial Psychology, 21*(1), 73–88.

Field, E.M. (2007). *Bully blocking.* Sydney, Australia: Finch.

Seligman, M.E.P. (1975). *Helplessness: On depression, development, and death.* San Francisco: W.H. Freeman.

Chapter 4

Janoff-Bulman, R. (1992). *Shattered assumptions: Towards a new psychology of trauma.* New York: Free Press.

Cuddy D.R., Cuddy, A.J.C., & Yap, A.J. (2010). Power posing: Brief nonverbal displays affect neuroendocrine levels and risk tolerance. *Psychological Science, 22,* 95–102.

Lutgen-Sandvik, P. (2008) Intensive remedial identity work: Responses to workplace bullying trauma and stigmatization. *Organization Articles, 15*(1), 97–119.

Chapter 5

Carney, D., Cuddy, A.J.C., & Yap, A. (2010). Power posing: Brief nonverbal displays affect neuroendocrine levels and risk tolerance. *Psychological Science, 21,* 1363–1368.

Dingfelder, S.F. (2010). Face-to-face communication captured by fMRI. *Monitor on Psychology, 41*(7), 11.

Field, E.M. (2010). *Bully blocking at work.* Brisbane, Australia: Australian Academic Press.

Kraus, M.W., Cote, S., & Keltner, D. (2010). Social class, contextualism and empathetic accuracy. *Psychological Science, 21*(11), 1716–1723.

Mehrabian, A. (1981). *Silent messages: Implicit communication of emotions and attitudes.* Belmont, CA: Wadsworth.

Chapter 6

Field, E.M. (2007). *Bully blocking*. Sydney, Australia: Finch.

Solomon, M. (2002). *Working with difficult people*. New York: Prentice Hall Press.

Chapter 7

Field, E.M. (2010). *Bully blocking at work*. Brisbane, Australia: Australian Academic Press.

Frankl, V.E. (1946). *Man's search for meaning*. New York: Simon and Schuster.

Rayner, C. (1997). *Bullying at work* (bullying survey report). London: Unison.

Soares, A. (2004, June). *Bullying, post-traumatic stress disorders, and social support*. Paper presented at the Fourth International Conference on Bullying and Harassment in the Workplace, Bergen.

Conclusion

Field, E.M. (1999). *Bully busting*. Sydney, Australia: Finch.

About the Author

Field, E.M. (1999). *Bully busting*. Sydney, Australia: Finch.

Field, E.M. (2007). *Bully blocking*. Sydney, Australia: Finch.

Field, E.M. (2010). *Bully blocking at work*. Brisbane, Australia: Australian Academic Press.

Bibliography

Adams, A. (1992). *Bullying at work: How to confront and overcome it.* London: Virago.

Babiak, P., & Hare, R.D. (2006). *Snakes in suits: When psychopaths go to work.* New York: Collins.

Clarke, J. (2005). *Working with monsters.* Sydney, Australia: Random House.

Crawshaw, L. (2007). *Taming the abrasive manager: How to end unnecessary roughness in the workplace.* Jossey-Bass Management Series.

Davenport, N., Schwartz, R.D., & Elliott, G.P. (1999). *Mobbing: Emotional abuse in the American workplace.* Ames, IO: Civil Society Publishing.

Einarsen, S., Hoel, H.Z.D., & Cooper, G.L. (2003). *Bullying and emotional abuse in the workplace.* London and New York: Taylor and Francis.

Einarsen, S., Hoel, H., Zapf, D., & Cooper, G.L (2011). *Bullying and harassment in the workplace* (2nd ed.) London and New York: Taylor and Francis.

Felder, L. (1993). *Does someone at work treat you badly?* New York: Berkley Books.

Field, E.M. (2010). *Bully blocking at work.* Brisbane, Australia: Australian Academic Press.

Field, E.M. (2007). *Bully blocking.* Sydney, Australia: Finch.

Field, T. (1996). *Bully in sight.* Leeds, UK: Success Unlimited.

Fineberg, L.S. (1996). *Teasing: Innocent fun or sadistic malice?* New Jersey: New Horizon Press.

Futterman, S. (2004). *When you work for a bully, assessing your options and taking action.* NJ: Croce Publishing Group

Graves, D. (2002). *Fighting back.* United Kingdom: McGraw Hill Professional.

Hare, R.D. (1999). *Without conscience, the disturbing world of psychopaths among us.* New York: Guilford Press.

Herman, J.M.D. (1997). *Trauma and recovery: The aftermath of violence from domestic abuse to political terror.* Basic Books.

Hockley, C. (2002). *Silent hell: workplace violence and bullying.* Adelaide, Australia: Peacock Publishers.

Horn, S. (2002). *Take the bully by the horns.* New York: St Martin's Press.

Hornstein, H. (1996). *Brutal bosses and their prey.* New York: Riverhead books.

Janoff-Bulman, R. (1992). *Shattered assumptions: Towards a new psychology of trauma.* New York: Free Press.

Marais, S., & Herman, M. (1997). *Corporate hyenas at work.* Pretoria: Kagiso Publishers.

Mathieson, S., Burns, J., & Hansen, M. (1998). *Safe and sound.* New Zealand: Top Drawer Consultants.

Namie, G., & Namie, R. (2009). *The bully at work.* Naperville, IL: Source Books.

Olsen, H. (2005). *Workplace bullying and harassment.* CCH New Zealand Ltd

Randall, P. (1997). *Adult bullying: Perpetrators and victims.* London: Routledge.

Richards, H., & Freeman, S. (2002). *Bullying in the workplace: An occupational hazard.* Sydney, Australia: Harper Collins.

Solomon, M. (1990). *Working with difficult people.* USA: Prentice Hall.

Sutton, R. (2007). *The no asshole rule, building a civilized workplace and surviving one that isn't.* New York: Warner Business Plus, Hachette books.

Tehrani, N. (2001). *Building a culture of respect.* London and New York: Taylor Francis.

Wyatt, J., & Hare, C. (1997). Work abuse: How to recognize and survive it. Rochester, VT: Schenkman Books.

About the author

Evelyn M. Field is a professional speaker, practising psychologist, best-selling author, regular media commentator on bullying and related issues on television, radio and print media, and Fellow of the Australian Psychological Society. She has extensive clinical, legal and personal experience in dealing with trauma, loss and abuse. She is known as an international professional expert in treating victims of school and workplace bullying, having specialised in this area for over 35 years.

Bully Busting (1999), Evelyn's first self-help book for parents, children and educators, sold over 23,000 copies and has been translated into Italian, Croatian and Arabic. Her follow-up, *Bully Blocking* (2007) — also a best-seller — has been translated into Czechoslovakian and Korean. The first part of her workplace books, *Bully Blocking at Work*, was released in 2010 by Australian Academic Press.

Currently Evelyn is investigating the unique impact of workplace bullying on the victim's psychological, social and physical health. Her research is revealing a common constellation of symptoms; this pattern or profile appears to differ from other victims of trauma, and she has named it Workplace Bullying Trauma (WBT). If her hypothesis is supported, this will help in diagnosis and treatment for all victims of workplace bullying.

Evelyn is on the Advisory Council of the National Centre Against Bullying (NCAB) and spent 5 years on the Board of VOCAL (Victims of Crime Assistance League, Victoria), 20 years as a Board Member of the Mental Health Foundation of Victoria, and 11 years as Honorary Secretary of the Australian Association for Mental Health.

Evelyn speaks regularly to schools and organisations, and became an Accredited Speaking Member of National Speakers Association; she has spoken in New Zealand, Belgium, Spain, the United States, Vietnam, Wales and Israel. She is regarded as a passionate speaker; her keynotes and workshops are entertaining, as well as ethical and educational. She uses a variety of techniques, including case studies, cartoons, magic and role-playing, to engage participants and help them develop new skills. The core of her training is based upon the six bully-blocking strategies derived from her personal and professional experience.

Evelyn is also one of the few experts worldwide who conduct approved professional development training programs for psychologists, psychiatrists and counsellors in treating targets of school and workplace bullying. She provides keynotes and workshops across Australia and overseas on the following topics:

- 'Respect and Resilience at Work: Managing Workplace Bullying and Harassment'
- 'Bully Blocking Strategies at Work'
- 'Managing Bullying at School: Developing Social and Emotional Resilience'
- 'Bully Blocking Skills for Students'
- 'Treating Victims of School or Workplace Bullying'.

For further information, contact Evelyn at efield@bullying.com.au or visit Evelyn's website at www.bullying.com.au

Acknowledgments

My special thanks to Paul McCarthy, who inspired me to write a book on workplace bullying over 12 years ago; thanks also to my many colleagues in Australia, especially the Australian Psychological Society and the Australian media, as well as the International Association for Workplace Bullying and Harassment (IAWBH), who provide me with intellectual validation, inspiration and encouraged me to achieve even more. Due to a lymphoma and years of rewriting and rejections, I am deeply grateful to Stephen May and Roberta Blake, who brought 12 years of intensive work to publication and helped me turn my bulky manuscript into two user-friendly books. It has been a deeply rewarding pleasure to work with them. I also have benefitted greatly from my office support team — my personal assistant, Inna Tranis, and postgraduate research assistant, Joanna Ponniah; as well as Patricia Ferris in Canada and Les Posen in Melbourne for their professional support.

Thank you to the many people who gave me their stories, my international and local professional colleagues, the inspiring international web support groups for victims of workplace bullying, and the many clients whom I can't name for confidential reasons.

Although I've tried to quote references appropriately, some information was lost during the extensive rewriting over many years. I hope that those who weren't acknowledged will understand.

Special thanks to: Alexander Ranoschy, Andrea Pilmear, Ann Wisniak, Anne Thompson, Arnold Zable, Anthony Grant, Barbara Guest, Barbara John, Berndatte Crompton, Bill Temple, Brian McAvoy, Bruce Fallaver, Carolyn Davies, Charles Goulding, Charlotte Raynor, Charmine E. J. Härtel, Colin Fraser, Cynthia Logan, David Field, Danielle Jelinek, David Griggs, D. Revell Thomas, Frederick Davidson, Gary Collis, George Halascz, George Norris, George Cooper, Graeme O'Neil, Guy Croyle, Hadyn Olsen, Helen Bourke, Helen Shardy, Helge Hoel, Miriam Kanat, Izaak Fried, Jacinta Di Mase, Jeff Lomas, Jens Karnoe, Jo Murphy, John and Jane Covey, Judy Bernshaw, Julie Ankers, Kalman Rubin, Katrina Hall, Kenneth Westhues, Kim Sawyer, Leon Gettler, Leonie Morgan, Louis Waller, Mark Williams, Maria Pena, Moira Adams, Michael Sheehan, Michael Tunnecliffe, Michelle Barker, Michelle Waddington, Michael Sput, Naomi Raab, Noreen Tehrani, Nicholas K. Stretch, Pamela Lutgen-Sandvik, Paddy Dewan, Patmalar Ambikapathy, Pam Kennedy, Rabbi and Mrs Shimshon Yurkewicz, Rex Finch, Richard Bennison, Rochelle Umansky, Ronnie and Tania Zohar, Robert Wood, Rosie Hughes, Sally Jetson, Sam Horn, Sarah Cornally, Sarah Rey, Stale Einarson, Susan E. Shaub, Susan Marais Steiman, Susan Mclean, Sue Davies, Sue Goss, Sue Hosking, Tim Field, and Winston Marsh.